# The Revolutionary Russian Economy, 1890–1940

T0330612

The Russian and Soviet experience of attempting to create a new type of economy is still inadequately understood by many. This book will increase our understanding of the actual conditions prevailing in both the pre- and post-revolutionary eras and why the decisions that were taken were made, as well as presenting alternative policy options for the reader to consider.

Fresh perspectives are brought to bear upon the revolutionary Russian economy in this book. Applying the ideas of orthodox economic theory, Marxism and also institutionalism, the volume encourages the reader to think critically about the development of the Russian/Soviet economy, and also examines the original theories of Russian economists of the period.

Intelligent writing, incisive insights and conceptual originality characterise Vincent Barnett's book and both economic and political historians will relish it.

**Vincent Barnett** is a Research Fellow at CREES, Birmingham University, UK. He is also author of *Kondratiev and the Dynamics of Economic Development*, one of the editors of Nikolai Kondratiev's collected works, and the author of numerous articles in Russian studies, economic history and history of economic thought journals.

# Routledge Explorations in Economic History

# The Revolutionary Russian Economy, 1890–1940

## Ideas, debates and alternatives

Vincent Barnett

Routledge
Taylor & Francis Group

LONDON AND NEW YORK

First published 2004
by Routledge
2 Park Square, Milton Park, Abingdon, Oxon, OX14 4RN

Simultaneously published in the USA and Canada
by Routledge
270 Madison Ave, New York NY 10016

*Routledge is an imprint of the Taylor & Francis Group*

Transferred to Digital Printing 2006

© 2004 Vincent Barnett

Typeset in Sabon by Wearset Ltd, Boldon, Tyne and Wear

*British Library Cataloguing in Publication Data*
A catalogue record for this book is available from the British Library

*Library of Congress Cataloging in Publication Data*
A catalog record for this book has been requested

ISBN10: 0–415–31264–7 (hbk)
ISBN10: 0–415–40698–6 (pbk)

ISBN13: 978–0–415–31264–6 (hbk)
ISBN13: 978–0–415–40698–7 (pbk)

# Contents

# Tables

# Acknowledgements

I have accumulated many intellectual debts over the years, too many in fact to list here in detail. I would however like to thank Rob Langham and Terry Clague at Routledge for being appreciative of my initial proposal for this book, and two anonymous referees for their useful suggestions. Three ESRC-funded projects on the history of Russian economic thought have provided me with the welcome and privileged opportunity of studying the work of various economists in detail. In particular the project entitled 'The Economic Mind in Russian Civilisation, 1880–1917' (R000239937) gave me the time necessary to complete this book. The Centre for Russian and East European Studies, Birmingham University, kindly provided the institutional framework for these endeavours.

I would also like to acknowledge a profound debt to two rather different intellectual traditions – Ancient Greek scepticism and American institutionalism – both of which at different times proved to be rather unlikely (yet very welcome) saviours of the mind. It is to the sceptical concept of *ataraxia* that I dedicate this book, hoping that it will bring some readers closer to the state of supreme mental tranquillity that, tradition has it, was actually achieved by Pyrrho of Elis (360–270 BC), through the skilful application of that magical instrument, the universal refuter.

# Timeline: Economic ideas and political events in Russia

|  | Key events in Russian history | Key developments in economic theory |
|---|---|---|
| 1861 | The emancipation of the serfs |  |
| 1867 |  | Marx's *Capital* (volume one) is published in German |
| 1870 |  | The marginal revolution in Western economics begins |
| 1871 |  | Sieber's *Ricardo's Theory of Value and Capital* |
| 1872 |  | The first Russian edition of volume one of Marx's *Capital* is published |
| 1881 | Marx issues a judgment on whether Russia must pass through capitalism and Alexander II is assassinated |  |
| 1884 |  | Jevons's *Investigations in Currency and Finance* |
| 1885 | Nobles Land Bank established | The second volume of *Capital* is published posthumously by Engels |
| 1887 | A plot to kill Alexander III is uncovered and Lenin's brother is executed |  |
| 1889 |  | Bohm-Bawerk's *Positive Theory of Capital*, Hobson's *Physiology of Industry* and Clark's *Distribution of Wealth* |
| 1890 | The first industrialisation drive in Russia begins | Keynes's *Scope and Method* and Marshall's *Principles of Economics* |
| 1891 | Tariff barriers on foreign imports greatly expanded |  |
| 1894 | Death of Alexander III and appointment of Nicholas II as the new Tsar | Tugan-Baranovsky's *Industrial Crises in Contemporary England* and the third volume of *Capital* is published by Engels |
| 1897 | Gold standard introduced |  |
| 1898 | RSDLP founded | Tugan-Baranovsky's *Russian Factory in 19th C.* |
| 1899 | An economic depression begins in Russia | Veblen's *Theory of the Leisure Class* and Lenin's *Development of Capitalism in Russia* |

|  | *Key events in Russian history* | *Key developments in economic theory* |
|---|---|---|
| 1904–1905 | Russo-Japanese war | |
| 1905 | The first Russian revolution | |
| 1906 | New Fundamental Laws for the Empire are issued | Fisher's *Nature of Capital and Income* |
| 1906–1911 | Stolypin's agrarian reforms | |
| 1908 | | Barone's 'Ministry of Production' |
| 1911 | | Fisher's *Purchasing Power of Money*, Schumpeter's *Theory of Economic Development* and Hilferding's *Finance Capital* |
| 1909–1913 | An industrial boom occurs in Russia | |
| 1913 | | Mitchell's *Business Cycles*, Luxemburg's *Accumulation of Capital*, Struve's *Economy and Price* and Keynes's *Indian Currency and Finance* |
| 1914–1918 | First World War | |
| 1915 | Russian gold begins to be transferred overseas in order to finance the war | Slutsky's 'On the Theory of the Budget of the Consumer' |
| 1916 | The issue of paper money continues to gather pace | Lenin's *Imperialism, the Highest Stage of Capitalism* |
| 1917 | February and October revolutions in Russia | Tugan-Baranovsky's idea of 'marginal planning' and Bogdanov's notion of 'war communism' are proposed |
| 1918–1920 | Civil war in Russia | |
| 1919 | | Bukharin's *Economics of the Transition Period*, Keynes's *Economic Consequences of the Peace* and Veblen's 'Bolshevism and the Vested Interests in America' |
| 1920 | | Pigou's *Economics of Welfare* |
| 1921–1929 | New Economic Policy | |
| 1921 | | Preobrazhensky's *Finance in the Epoch of the Dictatorship of the Proletariat* and Lenin's *The Tax in Kind* |
| 1923 | The scissors crisis, or the crisis of relative prices | Keynes's *Tract on Monetary Reform* |
| 1924 | The death of Lenin | Chayanov's 'On the Theory of Non-Capitalist Economic Systems' and Commons's *Legal Foundations of Capitalism* |

|  | Key events in Russian history | Key developments in economic theory |
|---|---|---|
| 1925 | Fourteenth Party Congress begins the shift away from NEP and towards planning | Chayanov's *The Organisation of Peasant Farms*, Groman's 'On Some Regularities ...', Pervushin's *Economic Conjuncture* and Kondratiev's 'Long Cycles of Conjuncture' |
| 1926 | Grain production recovers to pre-war levels | Bazarov's 'Curve of Development ...', Popov's 'Balance of the National Economy', and Preobrazhensky's *New Economics* |
| 1927 | 'War Alarm' and grain crisis occur | Slutsky's 'The Summation of Random Causes as the Source of Cyclic Processes' |
| 1928 | Party-orchestrated attacks against 'bourgeois' economists strengthen | Fel'dman's 'Towards a Theory of National Income Growth' and Yurovsky's *Monetary Policy of Soviet Power* |
| 1929 | Mass collectivisation of agriculture begins | |
| 1929–1933 | First five-year plan | |
| 1930 | | Preobrazhensky's *Theory of Depreciating Currency* |
| 1933 | | Ohlin's *Interregional and International Trade* and Frisch's 'Propagation Problems and Impulse Problems' |
| 1933–1937 | Second five-year plan | |
| 1936 | | Keynes's *General Theory of Employment, Interest and Money* |
| 1936–1938 | The Great Purges | |
| 1938 | Kondratiev, Bukharin, Yurovsky, Bazarov all murdered on Stalin's orders | Lange's *On the Economic Theory of Socialism* |
| 1939 | Outbreak of Second World War in Europe | Schumpeter's *Business Cycles*, Harrod's 'Essay in Dynamic Theory' and Kantorovich's *Mathematical Methods* |
| 1941 | Germany invades the USSR | Leontief's *Structure of American Economy* |

# 1 Introduction to Russian economy

I think it is a disaster for the idea of Planning that Russia should have been the country where it has first been tried out.[1]

## The aims of the book

The Russian and Soviet experience of attempting to create new types of economy is, perhaps surprisingly, still inadequately understood by both historians and economists. This is due to a number of factors – the Russian language barrier, cold war hostility, archaic forms of expression, difficulty in locating sources, the distorted priorities of ruling elites, incomplete conceptions of the subjects of history and economics themselves – to name but a few. This book aims to increase this understanding a little by providing an intermediate-level guide to the reality that unfolded, the debates which occurred and the alternatives which existed with regards to Russian economic development between 1890 and 1940, especially as economic thinkers conceived them at the time.[2] It utilises existing scholarship and published materials extensively – sometimes reinterpreting them – adding theoretical lucidity and employing new unpublished sources when this further enables understanding of the topic under examination. Originality is thus provided first of all in terms of approach, perspective and scope, with the important (but sometimes neglected) contributions of Russian economic theorists being considered at length. It is intended primarily to stimulate new thinking, rather than to enshrine empirical fact.

In general terms the book views both history and economics as subdisciplines of an over-arching subject defined loosely as the study of human social behaviour, or more specifically the large-scale or macro-consequences of individual human behaviour at specific points in space and time. It also takes a much wider view of the significance of 'economy' in general and the actual range of knowledge required in order to begin the process of understanding it. The book does not assume that one single principle guides all human behaviour at all times. Rather it accepts that various different principles and motivations guide this behaviour in

different places and at different times, these being partly culturally determined and partly genetically so in a continuous process of mutual interaction. Human behaviour is extremely varied and complex, and so are the
particular economic manifestations of this behaviour.

Nor does the book accept that there is any such as thing as 'the
economy' that can easily be understood by means of a single homogenous
'essence' that explains everything;[3] rather there are only various cascades
of 'economy' in all its multifarious forms and concrete specifics. The historically original manifestations of human behaviour in terms of economy
that occurred (or were allowed to occur) in Russia between 1890 and
1940 are the subject of this work. As this is a rather broad conception of
the subject under review, the reader will find that the book utilises a wide
range of work not always encountered in Russian history texts. This is
because in reality breadth is as important as depth to an understanding of
human affairs, everything being ultimately connected.

Moreover the book examines 'revolutionary Russian economy' in two
distinct but related senses. First, it analyses the economy of Russia in the
revolutionary period – very broadly defined as 1890 to 1940. It was a
'revolutionary' economy not just in relation to the political events of
1905, 1917, 1921 and 1929, but more significantly in relation to
various attempts at major industrial transformation from the time of
Sergei Witte to Joseph Stalin and also in respect of the creation of new
types of economic structures and mechanisms. Second, the book
examines revolutionary new types of economic thinking, i.e. the original
ideas of economists as to what a revolutionary change in the Russian
economic system might actually mean and how economic forces in
general are best comprehended theoretically. These two strands continu-
ously interacted in the period under review, resulting in a period of
world-historical significance for economic affairs. Indeed some post-
1940 international economic developments could be seen as simply the
unfolding of theoretical possibilities first conceived in outline in the
period in question.

## What is history?

E.H. Carr famously asked 'What is History?' One rather unconventional
answer is that absolutely everything is history, including all the infinite
number of historical possibilities that did not actually become manifest in
our own unique timeline. History may consist in part of a corpus of ascertained facts selected from the world that is everything that is the case, but
it should also involve consideration of how and why what is not the case
(but could conceivably be so) came to be excluded from the totality of currently existing states of affairs.[4] Such counterfactuals are not just academic
exercises but help to explain how what did actually occur was the outcome
of specific choices undertaken by various individuals such as politicians,

economists, army officers, union leaders, crusading campaigners, grudge-bearing assassins and so on.

The philosopher David Lewis has recently advocated the startling notion of a plurality of worlds, or modal realism, an idea that he supported by arguments of serviceability and fruitfulness. For example in one such alternate world, which actually existed but was completely separate from our own world, all swans were blue and Cardiff was a suburb of Newcastle.[5] Whilst not going as far as to suggest that such alternative worlds do actually exist, this book considers them rather as latent historical possibilities, for the purpose of enabling a greater understanding of the actualised historical process.

Consequently, this book in part attempts to reconstruct a few of such latent historical possibilities from among the many potential worlds with respect to the Russian and the Soviet economy between 1890 and 1940. It does so by understanding how historical actors at the time perceived the options open to them with respect to economic development policy and industrialisation strategy, these people being charged with strategy selection and implementation. It also highlights various competing interpretations of economic affairs, and attempts to demonstrate how ideas, events, policies, institutions and personalities interacted to form the nexus of possible alternative realities. How and why the actual path seen was manifest is certainly considered in detail, but in a less dogmatic fashion than is usual in more conventional accounts of Russian economic history.

For example, Carr cited the death of V.I. Lenin in 1924 as an example of an accident that modified the course of history, but then suggested that such incidents should not enter into any rational interpretation of history.[6] The approach taken in this book disagrees fundamentally with Carr's judgment on this matter, since such 'modifications' in the course of history are crucial to understanding why one path was taken and another forsaken. Alternative possibilities are part of the fabric of history just as much as Carr's corpus of (allegedly) ascertained facts. In the case of Lenin's death in 1924, this resulted in the neglect of his idea of basing future Soviet economic development simply on cooperatives. If Lenin had continued to live after 1924, then this might well have resulted in the realisation of a very different conception of a socialist economy than that promoted by Stalin. Thus the death of one man in itself was not historically significant, but the concomitant eclipse of an alternative view of Soviet development promoted by the highly respected founder of the USSR certainly was.

Carr himself was not particularly enamoured with the idea of historical alternatives, possibly because right-wing critics wanted to wish away the existence of the USSR itself. He wrote disparagingly on hypothetical counterfactuals:

> Suppose, it is said, that Stolypin had had time to complete his agrarian reforms, or that Russia had not gone to war ... or suppose that the

Kerensky government had made good, and that the leadership of the revolution had been assumed by the Mensheviks or the Social Revolutionaries instead of by the Bolsheviks ... one can always play a parlour game with the might-have-beens of history.[7]

In this book alternative conceptions of a socialist economy are examined, something that Carr might have been a little more sympathetic towards. The motivation of this is not necessarily anti-socialist, as Carr believed the motivation of those who examined alternatives to Bolshevism often was. Rather this approach attempts to establish whether and to what extent alternative conceptions of socialism itself were prevalent in Russia during the period under review, a completely legitimate topic for the intellectual historian, in order to place the Bolshevik experiment in its true context.

Another distinguishing feature is that the book every so often makes an effort to examine the topics in question from the point of view of three different traditions of economic analysis, yet provides no privileged meta-language narrative from which to rigidly police the 'correct' interpretation of the history in question. Indeed it recommends that any such meta-language narrative provided by one person for the unquestioning adoption of another should be treated with great suspicion, since it usually functions in the self-interest of specific groups or institutions, rather than that of every human being on the planet. Individuals must come to their own conclusions about the correct interpretation of history, this book being merely an aid for achieving this yet-to-be-accomplished goal for each individual who encounters it.

## Three traditions of economic analysis

In this book the strategic questions addressed will periodically be examined from three points of view. The first is orthodox (or neoclassical) economics, the second is Marxist theory, and the third is institutional or evolutionary economics. A very short summary of the main elements of each approach is provided below, albeit with some unavoidable simplifications. Each of these three traditions has an understanding of existing reality and prescriptions for creating a better future. Each particular period will in part be examined from these viewpoints, and readers will be left to decide for themselves which particular approach or combination of approaches is ultimately 'true', if any.

From the point of view of orthodox economic theory, the aim of economic activity is to best utilise existing scarce resources. Socially optimal combinations of production and consumption, capital and labour, are achieved through natural market mechanisms, with the state playing only a night watchman role, and distribution is also best achieved through markets. Unrestricted free trade promotes international economic development, which should be left to high-flying entrepreneurs, while industrial protection hinders growth. Progress occurs through unfettered individual initiative and the natural selection of the fittest human specimens to occupy the top management positions. Private companies are the most efficient organisations for manufacturing commodities, and prices are best set through free competition. Economic rationality is defined in terms relating to the maximisation of the production of consumer goods and service output, and the (capitalist) economy naturally tends towards an equilibrium state of balanced growth. People get what they deserve, i.e. wages reflect people's relative contributions to the economy, and consequently everything is right with the world ('the real is rational'). Key economists: Adam Smith, David Ricardo, Leon Walras, Alfred Marshall. Key philosophers: John Locke, Jeremy Bentham, J.S. Mill.

From the Marxist point of view capitalism is an exploitative mode of production composed of a small ruling class – which owns the means of production, distribution and exchange – and a vast army of workers, who own nothing except their own labour power. These workers are subsistence wage slaves forced to provide the surplus product for the gluttonous satisfaction of a very small minority. The state is simply the executive arm of the minority ruling class, and international economic development is hindered by imperialistic rivalry. Private companies reflect the irrational desires of the ruling class, and the law of value regulates prices. Historical progress occurs through conflicts between the forces and the relations of production, or between new technology and old class structures. Within capitalism the organic composition of capital increases over time, resulting in workers continually being replaced by machines, and capital accumulation functions as a systemic compulsion. The capitalist mode of production is seen as severely limiting to human potential, but as a necessary if transient stage of economic development. People do not get what they deserve, i.e. relative wages reflect the class structure, which was created in an initial period of violent plunder and which is reinforced by both the ideological state apparatus and the repressive state apparatus. Consequently, everything is wrong with the world ('the rational is not yet real'). Key economic theorists: Karl Marx, Freidrich Engels, V.I. Lenin, Rudolf Hilferding. Key philosophers: G.W.F. Hegel, G.V. Plekhanov.

From the institutionalist point of view economies are systems of power, control and mutual coercion, which operate through mechanisms such as markets and structures such as political and legal formations. Institutions, or socially constructed systems of belief and action, are the fundamental basis of all economic systems, but these evolve in piecemeal fashion over time. The state plays a mediating role between all the important actors in the economy, although it often reflects the existing structure of power. Economic doctrines and legal sanctions are just conventions which are conditioned historically and which are modified over time. Private companies are 'going concerns' which embody both technological and business knowledge, sometimes in non-harmonious fashion, and prices are fixed by administrative control. Historical progress occurs through the continual conflict between existing ceremonial patterns, or temporal-specific habits of thought, and new scientific and technological developments, which often clash with received conventions. People get what institutions allow, i.e. wages reflect historically conditioned conventions about the division of spoils between various interest groups. Consequently, some things are reasonable and some things are not reasonable in the world ('the real evolves pragmatically over time, but not necessarily into the rational'). Key economists: Thorstein Veblen, John Commons, Clarence Ayres, J.K. Galbraith. Key philosophers: C.S. Peirce, William James, John Dewey.

In terms of the consequences of adopting these different approaches, an example can be given in relation to conceptions of what markets actually are and what they actually do. In the neoclassical view markets are mechanisms and/or places in which the free interaction of supply and demand produces a tendency towards the creation of equilibrium prices, and through which the real demands of the consumer determines production priorities. On the other hand in the socialist view, markets are irrational and exploitative mechanisms through which workers are drained of surplus value, and by means of which capitalism first generates and then overcomes economic crises. In the institutionalist view markets are exchange mechanisms governed by historically conditioned rules of behaviour, and through which the existing system of power determines production priorities. Other conceptions of market mechanisms exist also. For example in the Austrian view markets are processes actuated by the interplay of the actions of many individuals, and are constituted primarily through local knowledge and skills. It will be seen in what follows that adopting one or other of these views of what markets are has important consequences for designing economic policy and also for creating new institutions to replace them, and this must be an important factor to consider when various alternatives are being discussed.

## The Russian economy in the eighteenth century

A background sketch of Russian economic history before 1890 is required as a base measure from which to gauge developments after this date. The two most important rulers in eighteenth century Russia were Peter the Great (1682–1725) and Catherine the Great (1762–1796). The main goal of Peter the Great has been identified as the 'Europeanisation' of Russia, and in the Petrine period large-scale manufacturing was first established in the Russian armaments industry (such as cannon foundries), together with economic self-sufficiency in iron production. Most-favoured-nation status was given to certain foreign states with respect to trading privileges, although protection was raised in relation to certain domestic manufactures. On the monarch's command St Petersburg became an opulent European-style city of palaces, gardens and impressive buildings that had been constructed on the bones of the labourers, masons and carpenters that had been summoned by Peter the Great to build the new capital, this being one of his most enduring achievements.

Under Catherine the Great a significant reform of the military and civilian obligations placed upon various population classes occurred, and trade and industry (which had formerly been the preserve only of the nobility and the merchants) began to open up to those from more humble backgrounds such as the serfs. Throughout the eighteenth century the Russian government played a major role in the economy with respect to arranging monopolies, setting customs duties, raising taxes and procuring goods and services through market means. Military campaigns were also highly significant, both politically and economically, with important wars being fought against Sweden, Turkey and Prussia that stretched the resources of Russia significantly. Indeed military demands were an important stimulant to economic development.

With regards to financial development, private banking capacity in Russia began on a new course with the organisation of a Bank for the Nobility in 1754, which was granted permission to accept deposits from private individuals only in 1770. In 1772 other institutions were allowed to accept deposits and grant loans also, further enabling the growth of the Russian economy. On the negative side production costs in Russia were often higher than for corresponding goods made in Western Europe, due to deficiencies in areas like transport networks, the availability of capital and a shortage of skilled labour. Even so overseas demand for Russian goods such as flax, hemp, linen, grain and leather grew significantly throughout the eighteenth century.

For the Russian state budget various taxes were levied such as a salt tax, a tax on alcohol and a poll tax (on males, peasants and townsmen only), the latter being the most important sources of government revenue. The two major elements of government expenditure were the administrative bureaucracy and the armed forces. Government deficits were usually covered by inflation and the printing press, and the fiscal system in effect redistributed wealth from the lower to the higher classes of Russian society.[8] In general Russia in the eighteenth century (and beyond) maintained a highly unequal distribution of wealth, power and status. This was usually justified by reference to religious and natural class division ideologies, which had been accepted and even internalised to some degree by many of those at the base of the social pyramid, although by no means all.

## The Russian economy in the nineteenth century

A key feature of the Russian economy in the eighteenth and nineteenth centuries was serfdom; both its prevalence before 1861 and its abolition after this date. Serfs were legally bound to the land and subject to the control of their lord, and they constituted the lowest class within the feudal system. They performed a labour service for the landowner (*barshchina*) and also made specific payments both in money and in kind to them (*obrok*). Serf labour had been used extensively by Peter the Great to build military capacity and to create St Petersburg itself, whilst in the latter part of the nineteenth century peasant emancipation provided a major impetus to the growth of the Russian market and to the transfer of labour from village to town.[9] Industry in the first decade or so after 1861 was characterised to an important extent by small handicraft production, often under the control of the particular distribution network involved. Before peasant emancipation the state, the nobility or merchants usually owned the larger industrial establishments, whilst after 1861 the growth of free artisans led to the more extensive development of capitalistic enterprise. The relative immobility of labour and goods was characteristic prior to 1861, and the economic life of the country was (in general) rather isolated and self-contained at this time.

Other key elements of the nineteenth-century Russian economy were the existence of collective forms of economy such as the peasant commune, the prevalence of a powerful land-owning class, the existence of peasant artisan manufacture, and the development of Russian factory industry, both indigenous and of external origin. Foreign investment in Russian industry was concentrated mainly in St Petersburg, whereas indigenous Russian capital was predominantly centred in Moscow. Within the peasant commune non-capitalist customs and practices prevailed to a large extent, whilst within the newly developing factory, capitalist work habits were found. For example, the peasant commune periodically redistributed land among members, whilst in the factory the so-called 'sweating system' and piecemeal rates of pay could be found.

In terms of the hereditary aristocracy that prevailed in nineteenth-century Tsarist Russia, 10 per cent of the agrarian nobility owned 75 per cent of all land in estates.[10] This was an important factor engendering both structural inertia in the economy and intense resentment in the polity. The interests of the new industrial entrepreneurs sometimes clashed with those of the old agrarian nobility, for example over customs policy, tariffs favouring the development of new industries. Crucially railways were constructed across large parts of Russia in the second half of the nineteenth century, linking previously inaccessible regions, this providing a major impetus to develop trade links further. State assistance was a very significant element in railway construction, with *laissez faire* losing ground to protection as the favoured ideology in government circles towards the end of the nineteenth century. Russian grain exports to the UK received a boost after the repeal of the Corn Laws in 1846, and the triumph of free trade ideas in Britain had at least some reverberations in Russia.

While nineteenth-century Russia has traditionally been regarded as 'backward' by many historians, this is only in comparison with the economically *avant-garde* elite of Western Europe: compared to (say) Central America in the nineteenth century it was rather futuristic. This is important to bear in mind, as the Russian experience of economic development was in various periods held up as a model for even less developed countries to emulate, revealing the relative and transient nature of the concepts of 'advanced' and 'backward'. Marxism initially saw itself as an ideology relevant only to more developed countries, and hence the apparent paradox of it being successful first in Tsarist Russia. The ideological contortions that were necessary in order to smooth over this incongruity are an essential part of the story of the revolutionary Russian economy.

## The importance of geography to Russian economy

In terms of the employment of the population, agriculture was by far the most important element of Russian economy throughout the nineteenth century. In turn, grain was the single most important output from agriculture, being used for domestic consumption (both human and livestock) and also for export. In the second half of the nineteenth century the sown area of grain production increased significantly, as did yields.[11] However, for a long period Russian agriculture often advanced more by extensive methods, cut and burn for example, rather than by intensification.

Geographically the Russian Empire was divided into a number of distinct regions such as the Central Black Earth region, the North West, the South West, and Siberia, agriculture being of great importance in the fertile soils of food producing areas such as the Central Black Earth region. Some large-scale industry was concentrated in belts of activity surrounding Moscow and St Petersburg such as the Central Industrial Region, where textiles predominated. Regarding other sectors of industry, coal mining was located in areas such as Donets, iron production was centred in the Ukraine and significant petroleum deposits were located in Baku.

Moreover Russia was a very sizable continental land mass with little coastline access to ports, except at remote locations such as Archangel, Astrakhan on the Volga, the Baltic and the Black sea, this having serious consequences for the development of trading routes. The soil, climate and geographical location of the various regions of Russia were of major significance in explaining the relative backwardness of agriculture in these areas, with long and severe winters often hampering the short growing season and drought and soil erosion affecting fertility.[12] In terms of industrial development, some have highlighted the absence of the legal basis of commercial law as transmitted through the cultural tradition of the codes of Ancient Rome as being especially significant, although others have documented the development of a specifically Russian legal system in detail.

## Industrialisation, growth and development

There are many different theoretical approaches to analysing economic development, economic growth and industrialisation. There is a classical model of economic growth, a neoclassical approach, a Keynesian model, a Marxist view, an institutionalist view and many other approaches that can be borrowed from economic theory and applied to economic history. For W.W. Rostow a basic relationship underlaid all discussions of growth, the output of an economy being determined by two over-riding factors, the size and productivity of the workforce and also of capital, the latter including all natural resources and knowledge. Human motivations governed the rate of increase of these two complex variables over time, such motivations not always being of purely economic origin.[13] Thus growth was a function of capital stock services, natural resources, the labour force, applied knowledge and the socio-cultural milieu in a process of continuous dynamic shifts toward a moving equilibrium position.

Population growth in Russia in the period under review was extensive. The population of the Russian Empire grew from 19 million people in 1762 to 35.5 million in 1800, to 73.6 million people in 1861 and finally to 165.1 million in 1914, partly due to territorial expansion but also as a result of a significant rise in the population of European Russia.[14] As a consequence agricultural sown area increased significantly, as did the production and consumption of key manufactured goods such as textiles and iron. However a relatively slow improvement in the level of skilled labour in the nineteenth century was a hindrance on growth, as was the sheer size of the territories of the Russian Empire and the large distances between key market regions. The Russian capital stock did increase significantly, in particular the stock of agricultural land and the level of private industrial capital. However, domestic trading institutions grew and evolved only gradually, due to hindrances provided by the administrative bureaucracy and a relative shortage of trading capital.

Going beyond Rostow's approach in theoretical terms, the classical model of economic growth involved land, labour and circulating capital only, competition ensuring that labour was allocated to different farms so as to equalise its marginal product. The dynamic forces were taken to be population growth and increases in the wage fund, and diminishing returns to land was assumed to operate.[15] In a well-known model formulated by Roy Harrod, what was called the warranted rate of growth of an economy should equal the full employment savings ratio, i.e. the proportion of income which was saved, divided by the marginal capital-output ratio (the value of capital goods needed for the production of an increment of output) as a necessary condition for continuous equilibrium growth. A separate natural rate of growth was determined by the rate of growth of the physical labour force plus labour productivity. The warranted and natural rates of growth must coincide if there was to be continuous full employment growth, something that would occur (within the framework of this model) only by chance. This approach thus accounted for cyclical patterns in the economy, as the two different rates of growth came into and out of synchronisation.

From this followed the application of a 'knife-edge' metaphor to Harrod's model and the importance of understanding the relation between savings and investment to Keynesian economics in general.[16] Whilst in the classical view savings and investment was balanced through changes in the interest rate, in the Keynesian approach saving was a function of income and the interest rate was the price of foregoing monetary liquidity. The actual scope of savings amongst the rural population in Russia through most of the nineteenth century was limited, but began to increase rapidly in the 1890s following changes in tax rates and rises in grain prices. By January 1914, Russian state savings banks contained 1830 million rubles in deposits, more than one quarter of this being of peasant origin.[17] As will be seen in the next chapter, some economists were particularly concerned about the level of domestic savings in Russia in the two decades before the outbreak of the First World War.

In contrast to classical and Keynesian models, the Marxist view of capitalist growth was much more historically orientated, explaining accumulation systemically and positing a rising organic composition of capital (or capital/labour ratio), a tendency for the rate of profit to fall and the increasing immiseration of the working class, eventually leading to crisis and systemic collapse. Marxists after Marx added a new monopoly phase of capitalism, one dominated by financial and banking interests, that would provide for some of the centralised mechanisms required for socialist control of the economy. In relation to the Russian economy as seen from a Marxist perspective, elements of both feudal and capitalist forms of economy existed after 1861, but their precise relationship was controversial. Whether capitalism was developing in Russia naturally and of its own accord, or was only being fostered as a foreign implant, or could never in fact develop at all, was a key point of difference for various political groupings.

From still another perspective, the institutionalist approach to economic growth pitted the pecuniary motivated business elite against the rationally motivated engineers, technological change being seen as the motor of growth but as being constantly hindered by outdated habits and customs. For institutionalists the capitalistic machine process would lead to monopolistic control through the profit motive rather than for community need. The Schumpeterian approach to growth added account of the periodic 'clustering' of entrepreneurship around new technological innovations, a fact that helped to engender cyclical patterns in the economy. In Russia habits and customs were particularly ingrained in peasant culture, whilst technological knowledge was often the remit only of foreign specialists working in Russia.

In David Ricardo's model of international trade, comparative advantage should determine a country's production specialisation, as this was the most efficient arrangement of multilateral exchange. If a specific country possessed a natural factor endowment advantage, for example rich mineral deposits, then this should be utilised in selecting actual manufacturing capacity. Recently however the mainstream dominance of the Ricardian framework for understanding the patterns of international trade has come under fire from the new trade theory and its emphasis on the ideas of increasing returns and market structure. If in the Ricardian view international trade resulted from differences in factor endowment, then in the new trade theory other reasons were given for international trade, namely the inherent advantages of specialisation and the benefits of being first in any new industry. Initially it appeared to some as if old-style protectionism had been vindicated by the new doctrine, but free trade orthodoxy soon reasserted itself in the mainstream academic literature.

There are also analytical tools which could be applied to the Russian experience that originated in various branches of economic history, concepts such as proto-industrialisation, the take-off, the stages of economic growth, the prerequisites for industrialisation, substitutes for the prerequisites, economic and technological revolutions and so on. Proto-industrialisation referred to a period before industrialisation proper began, but which provided some necessary but not sufficient priming elements. W.W. Rostow's five stages of economic growth provided a stylised breakdown of the various steps that he believed all countries had to follow whilst industrialising; these stages being a traditional society, the preconditions for take-off, the take-off, the drive to maturity and the age of high mass consumption. The take-off was the third stage where the rate of growth increased dramatically, investment rising from 5 per cent of national income to 10 per cent or more.[18] According to Rostow Russia began the process of creating the preconditions as far back as Peter the Great, this process accelerating significantly after the emancipation of the serfs in 1861. The take-off itself had begun by 1890, assisted by rises in grain prices and growing export demand. The Soviet five-year plans represented for Rostow the drive to maturity.

The prerequisites for industrialisation referred to a set of features allegedly required before industrialisation proper could begin. Alexander Gerschenkron suggested that one such prerequisite – agrarian reforms that enabled peasant mobility and allowed a growing industrial market and agricultural exports – was not consistent with the facts of all the countries under review. This led to the idea of substitutes for the prerequisites, or the notion that the prerequisites for industrialisation could be different in each country.[19] The first and second economic revolutions referred to the shift from hunting/gathering to settled agriculture and from agriculture to industrial production, the idea of a revolution signifying in this context a fundamental change in the productive potential of society as a consequence of changes to the stock of knowledge.[20] In general it will be found that some of these ideas can be applied to some aspects of Russian economic history, although none are complete on their own as an explanation for the observed multifarious pattern of development.

## Institutions versus technology

One element of (old) institutional economics was the continual tension between institutions and technology, or between existing patterns of social behaviour and new scientific developments. For example in Thorstein Veblen's view the vested interests of industry strove continually to preserve the existing institutional structure of power and thus their favoured social positions, whilst against them were pitted the carriers of new technological developments such as the engineers, who constantly strove to change patterns of production in line with innovative workmanship. For John Commons the working rules that enabled transactions to occur changed as technology and corporate organisation developed, thus allowing going business concerns to continue to function. According to Clarence Ayres the conflict between institutions and technology existed primarily in the realm of ideas, the rational forces of science being in continual conflict with the inherited (emotional) patterns of culture.[21]

Within this framework developments in the Russian economy can be viewed as a constant battle between the Westernising forces of science and its allies within capitalist innovation, and the conservative forces of feudalism and its associated deep-rooted semi-medieval patterns of organisation. On the other hand, from a rather different perspective the revolutionary forces for social change could be identified with worker and peasant organisations such as cooperatives, which may have employed new technology as far as was possible but which favoured more egalitarian structures of organisation and control. Producer, consumer and credit cooperatives were popular in Russia in the last quarter of the nineteenth century, their structures being primarily of socio-political rather than of technological inspiration. Whether and to what extent technological factors rather than concerns about social justice were a determining factor in general Russian economic development is in reality still an open question.

In empirical terms the transformation from feudal structures (as symbolised by the wooden plough) to capitalist machine technology in Russia began in the cotton and textile industries in the 1840s, although in the metallurgy sector outdated techniques still persisted into the 1890s. Advanced technology was sometimes utilised in the oil industry even though some older methods still lingered throughout the nineteenth century. Steam transport began to be employed in the 1840s, whilst the first significant boom in railway construction occurred in the 1870s. It was often the case that new technology was introduced in Russia only through foreign imports and was employed by foreign capital, and with the help of foreign engineers.[22] In general terms Russia nurtured first class individual scientific talent such as the chemist D.I. Mendeleev and the mathematician Nicholas Lobachevsky, but the practical embodiment of new scientific ideas in technology was a much more difficult endeavour in the Tsarist economy. For example the number of new patents issued in Russia in 1917 was only 24,992, as compared to over one million in the USA at this time, although the circumstances of war undoubtedly played a part in creating this contrast.

## Comparative economic systems

Another approach that has been used to try to understand the Soviet economy is systems theory, where the structure of business operation was seen as paramount. For example, Janos Kornai defined an economic system as composed of elements on three different levels. The uppermost level was institutions, such as the corporation or ministry; the second level was organisations, such as the plant or sales department within a firm; the third level was units, or non-divisible elements at the base of the structure.[23] Within this type of framework similarities between the Soviet economy and other national economies became apparent, as did specific structural differences. Kornai also distinguished between what was called the bureaucratic and the market coordination of economic affairs, the former involving vertical relationships, the latter horizontal relationships, as the basic difference between planning and *laissez faire*.[24] This can quickly be seen as overly simplistic, however, as markets can certainly encompass hierarchies and bureaucratic institutions can sometimes engage horizontally with market agents in mixed economic systems.

For some commentators at least, socialist economy could be classed as 'goal-rational authority', in which central planners had the right to appropriate the economic surplus and distribute it on the basis of claimed teleological rationality. The question of how the planners were chosen and controlled then becomes a very important issue, as does how they prioritised various different goals. For others, Soviet-type economies were defined as being a system where an immense public corporation had monopolised all productive activity. The individual enterprise only received orders and did not bargain with other economic units, whilst planners were influenced by various politically set criteria such as rapid growth or income equality.[25] Within socialist economic systems some distinguished between centralised and decentralised socialism, the degree of centralisation relating to the range of alternatives open to subordinates in an organisation. In general the idea of comparative economic systems was useful in understanding Soviet-type economies, but was itself the product of a particular conceptual slant; what particular features to be selected for analysis was the key question, alternatives always being conceivable to those that were actually highlighted.

## Philosophical currents in Russia

In both the frameworks adopted in this book and in the period under review, philosophical matters were of major concern to social and economic theorists. Marxism employed a bowdlerised Hegelianism, classical and neoclassical economics claimed affinity to philosophical liberalism and utilitarianism, whilst institutionalists looked to pragmatism and Darwinian evolutionism for support. However in Russia between 1890 and 1940 the philosophical absences were as significant as the presences. Pragmatism had made very little headway by 1917, English liberalism was only moderately more prevalent among some social groups, and although Darwin was celebrated for his theory of natural selection, evolution applied to the economy was a strictly limited taste. Behavioural psychology became important to institutionalists but can be seen as a polar opposite to Hegelian essentialism, at least from the point of view of conventional logic.

For Hegelians like Marx, truth arose out of a contrast between opposites, or through a process of the clashing of alternate views, the class struggle between workers and capitalists being one such immanently determined process. However for pragmatists like C.S. Peirce the essence of belief was the establishment of habit, truth being closely related to convention, and hence there was no necessity about the outcome of the contingent and socially conditioned search for knowledge. Pragmatism was an indigenous American tradition and whereas European philosophy easily made the journey into Russia, US currents had a longer and more difficult passage into pre-revolutionary Russia. English possessive individualism, as epitomised by John Locke's conception of property rights and its basis in the idea of 'mixing' human labour with inanimate objects in the process of acquisition, was also never fully at home in the much more communitarian-based Russian tradition.

One particularly Russian philosophical phenomenon was the two opposing groups of Slavophiles and Westernisers, the former favouring indigenous Russian currents in religion and conservative philosophy, the latter looking to the West for inspiration and favouring more progressive views. However, both groups were German-oriented in philosophical outlook, aping to some extent the right and left Hegelian divide that had developed after Hegel's death. In relation to the revolt against metaphysics, the positivist emphasis on facts and scientific understanding gained some influence in Russia at the end of the nineteenth century. The neo-Kantian emphasis on the ethical foundations of human action was also popular in moderate socialist circles, but not amongst Marxists of the Social Democratic type.

Lenin's early philosophical work *Materialism and Empirio-Criticism* of 1908 revealed much about the underlying world-view held by some Marxist revolutionaries in Russia before 1917. This book was a sustained and at times vicious attack on philosophical relativism, as represented by George Berkeley, Ernst Mach, A.A. Bogdanov and many others, whose views on the theory of knowledge Lenin characterised as idealism. Ostensibly supporting philosophical materialism but also employing a version of the correspondence theory of truth, Lenin set about attempting to show how various Russian socialists had distorted Marx's ideas, for example by claiming that social being and social consciousness were identical, when in fact consciousness simply reflected being.[26] In the book Lenin also placed American pragmatism in the same boat as idealism, which was presented as the sworn enemy of genuine Marxism. Lenin's absolute conviction that his interpretation of the epistemological questions under review was correct, even against acknowledged 'greats' in the history of philosophy such as Berkeley, gave the lie to the authoritarian and rigid conception of truth on which his beliefs were really based, in contrast to the more inclusive conceptions provided by either the coherence or the pragmatic theories of truth, and philosophical relativism in general.

## The unique economy of Russia

Before 1890 Russia had developed some unique types of economy that were not simply copies of economic formations found overseas. For example the labour *artel* (or association) was a voluntary combination of individuals brought together for a specific industrial undertaking, often temporarily, which was controlled through joint management and responsibility.[27] Cooperatives were also extensively developed in Russia from 1865 onwards in forms such as consumer and agricultural societies and savings and loan associations. While cooperation in itself was not unique to Russia, the peasant commune (*mir*) was a very significant and original indigenous institution, with communal ownership of land and collective decision-making regarding overall policy. The Russian word for the commune – *mir* – also meant 'the world' and 'peace'.

Within the peasant commune agricultural land was divided into strips or parcels that were cultivated by individual households, but on a crop rotation system often determined collectively. These strips of land were periodically redistributed in accordance with demographic changes. A particular spatial pattern of village settlement dominated, with rows of residential dwellings constructed alongside the main village road but separated from the cultivated fields.[28] This pattern of settlement enabled mutual protection from outside influences and encouraged social interaction amongst households, but has been criticised from a purely economic perspective as being an inefficient use of the land, due to lack of incentives for soil improvement. Various other drawbacks, such as the over-use of common land and the economic consequences of both narrow strips and distant fields, have also been identified.

Not everyone was favourably disposed to this type of peasant organisation. The village commune was accused by some of promoting lawlessness and of being controlled by Bacchus, i.e. promoting alcoholism, and by others of being presided over by 'village tyrants' who acted as grabbers of land, money, and goods. Such accusations usually emanated from landowners who had been the subject to the type of primitive justice some-times meted out by the commune.[29] Moreover the commune was not a static institution, but one subject to change and development within itself, for example in relation to how and on what principle the periodic redistri-bution of land actually occurred.

In Russian manufacturing industry the workforce recruited from the peasantry was sometimes composed of associations of fellow countrymen (*zemlyachestvo*), a group of people from the same village or area who ven-tured off to work in industry together. This practice served to preserve peasant culture and helped to insulate individuals from the harshness of urban life. Russian students also formed such communitarian groupings. In the manufacturing sector of the economy, handicraft (*kustar*) produc-tion was prevalent in many industries, which entailed village artisans working for a wide market through an intermediary, for example in the making of boots, sheepskin and wool products, silk fabrics and enamel goods. The origin of *kustar* industry was connected to the rural position of serfs, who sometimes produced articles for noble consumption, but *kustar* production came to be used by capitalists in a decentralised system of control and distribution.

## Marx and Engels on socialist economy

What was the ultimate purpose of a socialist economy? For Marx the underlying rationale for supporting socialist ideas was to build a society where everyone could freely develop their individual species-being, or their need to express themselves artistically and emotionally through work, pleasure and personal relationships. Capitalism hindered this process significantly by restricting human potential by means of enforcing monoto-nous and uncreative work, allowing for very little leisure time, and encour-aging stunted human relationships mirroring the exploitative and miserly culture of the workplace. In socialist economy all human potential would be encouraged and developed, which would result in many more people reaching the creative heights of a Goethe, a Shakespeare, or a Marx. While this might sound rather utopian and optimistic, especially given the selfish depravities to which the human animal has proved itself capable of in certain circumstances, it must be the ultimate measure by which any socialist system claiming inspiration from Marx is finally judged.

In more specific terms Marx had distinguished between two stages of a post-capitalist society, socialism and communism, together with a transi-tional dictatorship of the proletariat. In communist society the guiding principle would be 'from each according to their ability, to each according to their needs', i.e. people would have all their needs satisfied regardless of their contribution, whilst in socialism people would be remunerated according to the actual amount of their work. Thus material abundance would likely be required for full communism to be achieved, although certainly not for the first stage of socialism. The dictatorship of the proletariat would be a transitional era in which the interests of the working class would be enforced directly by the state apparatus under communist political control, before the state itself as a separate institution withered away and the interests of each merged into the interests of all.

In addition Engels had predicted that the division of labour that predominated under capitalism would eventually disappear in socialism. In fact the fossilised specialisation of the capitalist mode of employment (he believed) was actually redundant even from a technical standpoint, as new machinery had altered the function of the labourer fundamentally.[30] Hence socialism would unlock the true potential of the new technology that had first been created by means of private capital. With respect to the techniques to be employed in the socialist planning process, very little had been outlined by either Marx or Engels, both preferring to provide only a general outline of purpose rather than a detailed account of specifics. Some might interpret this absence as telling.

## Other conceptions of socialist economy

Marx and Engels were not the only radical thinkers before 1917 to provide some guidance as to what a future socialist society might be like. This was advice that could have been employed in Russia after 1917 if it was so desired, and if those in control were not sometimes afflicted with rigidly coagulated thinking. For example socialists like Pierre Joseph Proudhon and Robert Owen and anarchists such as Peter Kropotkin had discussed this topic at length, although many Marxists had subsequently criticised and even dismissed much of their work as unscientific.

Proudhon, for example, outlined a view of anarchical socialism based upon ideas such as sincerity in exchange, the submission of capital to labour, the setting of interest rates to zero, and the equality of social position. Advocating the creation of new industrial institutions based on mutuality and federalism, Proudhon placed the moral foundation of social economy centre-stage and rallied against the pretensions of rank, title and honorific distinction. He also suggested an idea for a new type of bank based on bilateral credit, where people would mutually pledge each other their produce on the basis of equality in exchange, thus overcoming the need for interest as a category of economy. Kropotkin on the other hand envisaged an anarchistic communism in which the combination of husbandman and the mechanic, i.e. agriculture and industry, and the integration of mental and physical labour would be the ultimate goal pursued. In the UK H.M. Hyndman's idea of industrial communism was built on a model of the state-controlled postal service, in which each department of industry would become part of a giant cooperative system of control and distribution. Goods of all kinds would be warehoused in state stores for the genuine service of all, rather than only the privileged few.

Mainstream Western economists such as Leon Walras should also be considered under this topic heading. Walras's set of mathematical equations defining a general equilibrium state of perfect competition has been interpreted by some as a model of a future utopian society, rather than a description of any actually existing capitalist economy. Indeed Enrico Barone's 1908 article on 'The Ministry of Production in the Collectivist State' argued that the imputation rules for a socialist and capitalist economy were fundamentally the same, and hence that rational price formation was a rule-based process which was not bound only to market-control systems of power. Few Bolsheviks discussed Barone's work prior to 1917, or even after this date, and if they did, then very likely they dismissed it as being petty-bourgeois. The story of the return of the repressed notion of an economic optimum is part of the story that will unfold in what follows, as is the continued repression of alternatives to Bolshevik ideas after 1917.

## Conclusion

Various general aims and methodological concerns have been outlined thus far, together with short sketches of relevant theoretical doctrines and empirical background descriptions of aspects of Russian history before 1890. A flavour of some of the various different approaches to understanding both history and economics has also been given, which should be kept very much in mind as the book unfolds. In the next chapter a much more detailed account of how the Tsarist economy was developing in the decade and a half before the Bolsheviks assumed control of Russia is provided, with one (mind's) eye focused on structural concerns, one on theoretical innovations and a third on empirical spatial and temporal comparison.

# 2   Tsarist economy, 1890–1913

## The *belle époque* in Europe and America

The *belle époque* was a period in which revolutionary discoveries and ideas were being developed in many different fields of human activity and an air of optimism was generally prevalent across Europe and America, at least amongst ruling elites. It witnessed the manufacture of some of the most beautiful decorative jewellery so far created – that of Carl Faberge in St Petersburg – aimed at a privileged super-rich clientele. New movements in painting, music and design – such as impressionism and *art nouveau* – sprung forth majestically from the Victorian surround. The first *Tyrannosaurus rex* fossil was discovered in the USA in 1902, while in 1905 the then-patent clerk Albert Einstein's remarkable paper 'On the Thermodynamics of Moving Bodies' quickly ushered in the (special) relativity revolution. This placed subjective human perception, rather than an all-powerful God or impersonal natural forces, at the centre of the knowable universe.

Furthermore, discontinuity physics emerged in the work of Einstein and Max Plank, and Niels Bohr developed what today is known as the 'old' quantum theory and a new model of structure of the atom. Epistemology was replaced as the central component of modern philosophy by logic through the pioneering work of Gottlob Frege and Bertrand Russell. G.E. Moore's *Principia Ethica* of 1903 argued that 'good' was a simple, non-definable concept that could not be expressed in other terms, the meaning of which was innately given. Marie Curie discovered radioactivity in 1898, Markov chains were conceived and mouldable plastics such as bakelite were first manufactured. And the development of new forms of mass media such as photography and moving pictures began to shape popular culture and usurp the power of the printed press. Many of these new developments had profound significance for the century that followed, even if this significance was not always that which was initially foreseen by those who were involved in making the new discoveries.

In relation to economic development the *belle époque* was a period of great industrial transformation. Various important technological innovations in transport and communications that were occurring in Europe and the US coincided with the end of a prolonged economic depression, and previously 'backward' countries such as Italy, Japan and Russia were experiencing the beginnings of rapid growth.[1] The economist Joseph Schumpeter suggested that, for the period from the 1840s to the end of the 1890s in political terms, the interests and attitudes of the industrial and commercial classes controlled policies and many manifestations of culture, in a sense that could not be asserted for any preceding or subsequent period.[2] The end of the long nineteenth century witnessed the final flowering of 'bourgeois' power and culture before the revolutionary storm first broke.

In terms of economic theory in Western Europe the period 1890–1914 was characterised by the further strengthening – perhaps even the victorious triumph – of the new marginalist approach to economic theory that had arrived in the 1870s through the work of W.S. Jevons and Leon Walras, as witnessed by the mainstream dominance of Alfred Marshall in the UK. Important new contributions to economics were also made in the field of monetary theory by Irving Fisher and Knut Wicksell, and in the field of capital theory by Eugen von Bohm-Bawerk, the latter also providing a significant critique of Marx's economic schema. Fisher's work on the net present value concept was certainly original although it was not really seen as central to the foundations of economics, at least at the time of its first publication. Fisher's doctoral thesis on mathematics and value theory was also an important contribution to the foundations of economics.

In addition this period witnessed the growth of empirical and statistical economics, as exemplified by Wesley Mitchell's *History of the Greenbacks* of 1903, and the birth of American institutional economics as a contrapuntal alternative to orthodoxy. Perhaps the culmination of the *belle époque* in empirical economics was Mitchell's quarto *Business Cycles* of 1913, which attempted an integration of the theoretical explanation of cycles with a detailed statistical description of them. What was particularly original in Mitchell was the attempt to synthesise previously separate components and the detailed analysis of statistical data, rather than any profoundly original theoretical invention. Moreover institutional economics was created on the cusp of the new century in the work of Thorstein Veblen and his partly satirical *Theory of the Leisure Class* of 1899. Veblen introduced concepts such as conspicuous consumption, status emulation and the pecuniary canons of taste into economic thinking, and argued that arbitrary conventions and caste-signifying fashions were much more important than had previously been acknowledged in determining individual economic behaviour. Veblen achieved a certain level of fame amongst some sections of the population, but many mainstream economists did not take his work at all seriously.

## The *belle époque* in Russia

In many areas of intellectual pursuit Russia participated to a very important extent in the international developments that occurred during the *belle époque.* This is particularly true in the natural sciences and the arts. For example the line of eminent Russian mathematicians, P.L. Chebyshev, A.A. Markov and A.M. Lyapunov produced work of international renown in the field of probability theory, such as that on the law of large numbers and the central limit theorem, constituting an important school of mathematics in St Petersburg. In particular Chebyshev's theorem was described enthusiastically by J.M. Keynes as beautiful and so valuable that he quoted it in full in his *Treatise on Probability*, and the incredible prices realised today by even minor pieces from the Faberge workshop need no additional publicity.[3] Faberge was however (an outlying) part of a larger renaissance of Russian art that occurred at the end of the nineteenth century.

A new artistic movement was born in Russia in the 1890s called 'World of Art' that opposed nationalistic pan-Slavic ideals, looking instead to the past cultural traditions of Europe for inspiration. This movement included artists, writers, musicians, theatrical workers and even industrial designers and was centred overwhelmingly in St Petersburg, Russia's European bridgehead. Igor Stravinsky's ballets such as *The Firebird* and *The Rite of Spring* heralded a new jagged neoclassicism in musical theatre, whilst the psychologically studied plays of Anton Chekhov quickly became popular both in Russia and the West. There is little doubt that Russian artists and scientists were in the vanguard of new international developments at this time.

However in important areas of the social sciences it often seemed that Russia never fully managed to keep abreast of new developments, or received them in a peculiarly distorted form, the classic example being Marxism. While in Western Europe the genuine insights that Marxism contained were being incorporated into the ideology of the mainstream labour movement, in Russia a highly literal, blinkered and absolutist form of Marxism gained momentum, a development that would eventually have quite tragic consequences. It has often been assumed that economic theory generally in Russia suffered similarly from impoverishment by being isolated from developments in the West. However, the work of the Russian economists examined in this book will suggest that this was not always true, or that it became true only subsequent to the 1917 revolution, or appeared to be true only in retrospect. In fact Russian economics was a healthy and vibrant discipline in pre-revolutionary Russia, displaying many of the positive and negative characteristics of its Western counterpart. This should become apparent from the rest of this book.

## V.I. Lenin and the development of Russian capitalism

Within the general backdrop of the *belle époque*, Marxist ideas took fertile root in Russia. Perhaps the most significant economic work of unquestionable Marxist inspiration published in Russia after 1890 was Lenin's *Development of Capitalism in Russia* of 1899. In this lengthy work Lenin attempted to establish that Russia was already a capitalist country in that a domestic market had been created for Russian goods, a peasant bour-geoisie and proletariat were forming, and modern machine industry had created a division of labour that clearly separated workers from peasants.[4] Lenin defined the process of the formation of a home market as simply the development of the social division of labour – such as the differentiation of the peasantry – and the degree of development of the home market was seen as the extent of development of capitalism itself. The creation of a domestic market proceeded by the conversion of the means of production into fixed capital and the means of subsistence into variable capital, foreign markets not being required necessarily for the realisation of surplus value.[5] Lenin saw the market itself as a category of commodity economy that only gained universal prevalence under capitalism, a doctrinal dissoci-ation that would prove useful many years later when Lenin introduced the New Economic Policy in 1921.

However, the significant amount of foreign investment in the Russian economy and the importance of specifically Russian institutions such as the peasant commune were glossed over by Lenin as they did not suit the aim of his analysis; to demonstrate that capitalism was developing in Russia indigenously and of its own accord. Lenin suggested that the system of relations in the community village did not constitute a special economic formation, this being in contrast to many who had investigated it, but instead were an ordinary petty-bourgeois type of economy containing exploitation. A significant number of Lenin's socialist contemporaries dis-agreed with this analysis, suggesting instead that capitalism was only developing in Russia as a foreign implant, and indeed much evidence could be mustered for such a view. This was a crucial question for revolutionar-ies given that their current political strategy (allegedly at least) flowed rationally from their social and economic analysis. If capitalism was devel-oping in Russia through the formation of a home market then its 'mission' was indeed partly progressive, but also it brought with it profound contra-dictions in the form of social differentiation and the most exploitative forms of capitalism such as those in the handicraft industry. According to Lenin his opponents downplayed such matters in their idealisation of indigenous Russian traditions, and the development of capitalism in Russia should neither be ignored nor idealised. It will be seen that the underlying assumptions made in Lenin's analysis had important consequences for later developments in Russian socialism.

## The imperial Russian government

One of the most important constraints on pre-revolutionary Russian intel-lectual development was the system of government that ruled Imperial Russia in the decades before the First World War. The monarchical auto-cracy that dominated required that individual government ministers reported to the Tsar directly, the monarch having the absolute right to dismiss ministers at will. This system sometimes resulted in a lack of coordination between different ministries and even ministries pursuing contradictory goals on specific issues.[6] At the turn of the century Tsar Nicholas II had been accused of being more concerned with private family matters than with designing policies that would lead Russia successfully into the new industrial age. Consequently the state bureaucracy sometimes acted from career advancement motivations rather than from strategic considerations of overall benefit to the Russian nation.

One evaluation of the dilemmas facing the government authorities in 1888, provided in a British Consul-General report, described them as constituting the political aspects of Russian economic conditions. There were said to be two opinions as to the necessity of the centrally orchestrated interference in local and municipal self-government that had recently been occurring. One was critical, suggesting that this hindered the development of institutions that might form a basis for a future parliamentary form of government, while the other was positive, suggesting that without such interference the corruption and disorder that was already manifest would be heightened. The Consul-General observed that:

> These opposite opinions divide the intellectual or educated classes into those who advocate a pursuance of the *laissez-faire* system, and those who maintain that direct and strong intervention in Local Government can alone save the country ... The Central Government is visibly imbued by the latter opinion, and ... is rapidly reassuming the administration of the country in its most minute local details.[7]

As the reverence of the peasantry for the Tsar was apparently unshaken even by oppressive taxes and grinding poverty, there was little to impede the extension of absolute government that was said to be occurring at this time.

Various attempts at both economic and political reform did occur between 1880 and 1913, although these attempts were usually reactive, sometimes half-hearted and at best only partially successful. For example following the revolutionary events of 1905 a legislative parliament was created – the Duma – but the Tsar resented the constraints that this imposed on his autocracy.[8] When the Duma came to be dominated by the Kadet party the government simply took illegal action to reduce peasant representation. Between 1906 and 1911 a series of agricultural reforms were introduced by Peter Stolypin that attempted to encourage peasants to move from communal forms of agriculture to privately owned farms. The aim was to create a class of prosperous peasant landowners who would increase agricultural productivity, but while these reforms had some success, their take-up was less than had been hoped for and at a slower pace than had been predicted. Stolypin underestimated the durability of traditional Russian institutions such as the peasant commune, just as Marx had initially done before him.

Joseph Schumpeter's analysis of Russian absolutism is also worth considering at this point. He suggested that in Russia a bureaucratic and military despotism was superimposed on peasant democracy, and that Tsarist expansionism rested more on Germanic and Mongol elements within the Empire than on Slavic ones. Moreover, military aggression was an essential part of the mind-set of the sovereign for reasons more of prestige maintenance rather than rational self-interest.[9] It is certainly true that irrational considerations played a major role in determining the policies pursued by the Tsar, although some type of reasoning usually had its place as well, and that a mixture of various community constituents often clashed within the Russian expanse. Overall the Imperial governmental structures have usually been seen as a hindrance to progressive economic developments within Russia, although many intellectuals managed to produce work of great merit nonetheless.

## Key Russian economists of the period

The most significant Russian/Ukrainian economic thinkers and policy-makers of the period included: M.I. Tugan-Baranovsky, P.B. Struve, Sergei Witte, A.I. Chuprov, P.A. Stolypin, V.I. Lenin, N.N. Shaposhnikov, V.K. Dmitriev, I.Kh. Ozerov, V.N. Kokovtsov, V.P. Vorontsov, D.I. Mendeleev and P.L. Bark. Tugan-Baranovsky was famous for pioneering work on trade cycle theory and for his account of the history of the Russian factory. Struve was well known as the leader of the 'Legal Marxist' grouping and for his book *Economy and Price*. Witte was famous as the architect of a state-assisted industrialisation programme for Russia. Stolypin was known for a series of agricultural reforms that attempted to replace communal landowning with capitalist farming. Lenin was famous (as an economist) for his rather selective analysis of the development of capitalism in Russia and for his account of imperialism as the highest stage of capitalism. Shaposhnikov worked (before 1917) on foreign trade policy and on the theory of value. Dmitriev pioneered the introduction of mathematical economics into Russia. Kokovtsov was Minister of Finance at various times between 1904 and 1911. Vorontsov opposed the development of capitalism in Russia against the views of economists such as Tugan-Baranovsky. Mendeleev supported protectionist policies and designed the 1891 tariff. And Bark was Minister of Finance during the First World War. Various aspects of the work of these economists will be considered in the following sections of this chapter, together with some of the policies and events that were connected to their lives and activities.

## Currents in economics in pre-revolutionary Russia

A number of different currents in political economy coexisted, and even interacted to some extent, in pre-revolutionary Russia. Perhaps the dominant current was historical political economy, followed by socialistic and then classical economics. The ideas of the German historical school were very influential in Russian universities, in particular the work of Wilhelm Roscher and Gustav Schmoller, through the teachings of their Russian disciples such as I.K. Babst, A.I. Chuprov and I.Kh. Ozerov. That the Russian economy was very different in general type and constituent structure from the British economy meant that any views stressing the importance of historical specificity to an understanding of economic development had great resonance amongst Russian intellectuals. Socialist economics, whilst akin to historical economics in some respects, differed significantly in relation to its prescription for radical change, historical sympathisers usually preferring to advocate piecemeal reforms only, rather than revolutionary overthrows of everything.

As an example of someone with historicist leanings, Alexandr Ivanovich Chuprov (1842–1908) was a very eminent Russian economist, lecturing on political economy at Moscow University and eventually becoming president of the Statistical Department of the Moscow Juridical Society. Chuprov had been sent to Germany as part of his education programme, returning to Russia in 1874, and thus he had first-hand experience of the home state of historical economics. In three 'Letters from South Germany' sent to the journal *The Russian Register* in 1873, Chuprov noted various similarities between living conditions in Bavaria and those in some regions of Russia, and suggested that it would be very difficult to identify another part of Western Europe where the conditions of economic life approximated so closely to those in Russia. As a student of I.K. Babst, Chuprov recognised that Babst had played a leading role in introducing the work of the German historical school into Russia. In 1869 Chuprov took various examinations in political economy that had been set by Babst, one of which was concerned exclusively with the historical school and its main representatives. In general Chuprov can be viewed as a leading proponent of Russian historical economics.

In respect of classical economics in Russia, the works of Adam Smith were well known and influential particularly in government circles, although Smith was employed only selectively, when circumstances were particularly amenable to it. David Ricardo's works were also known but perhaps less so than Smith's, due in part to Ricardo's very abstract and anti-historical approach. The protectionist ideas of List were quite popular amongst those in charge of industry and also in some sections of government, Russia often seeming comparable to Germany with regards to the degree of its industrial progress.

Marxism was also an important current in Russian political economy, although certainly not the dominant one, with the first Russian edition of volume one of *Capital* appearing in 1872. Following this publication a dispute arose within Russian Marxism about the relevance of the material-ist conception of history – the economic base of society determining the political and legal superstructure – to the particularities of the Russian situation. Marx himself eventually came to realise the importance of the unique and non-reductive nature of Russian institutions such as the peasant commune, although Russian Marxists at the end of the nineteenth century did not always fully share this understanding. A particularly econ-omistic interpretation of Marx often dominated in socialist debates, in part conditioned by the lack of access to the more 'humanistic' elements of Marx's writings, which had yet to be published at this time. In general a number of different currents in political economy flourished in pre-revolutionary Russia, elements of which will be examined in more detail as this chapter proceeds.

## V.K. Dmitriev and monopoly in Russia

Taking a much more analytical approach than historicists like Chuprov, V.K. Dmitriev has been called Russia's first mathematical economist. In the second study on Cournot's theory of competition from his *Economic Essays* of 1904, Dmitriev attempted to demonstrate that monopolistic forms of economy were not necessarily less efficient than free competition. He argued that if a monopolist used the same production techniques as those employed by competing entrepreneurs, then when monopoly pre-vailed, the national economy as a whole would not lose anything, since what was taken from the consumer through higher prices would be at the disposal of the monopolist. For Dmitriev in the competitive battle for sales, accumulating stocks of commodities played the same role as a mili-tary arms race between opposing powers did during peacetime. Under free competition the non-productive expenditure on commodity storage was higher than under monopoly, due to the need for competing producers to maintain significant levels of dead stock, in fear of others stepping in and gaining market share. Hence free competition (at least as modelled by neo-classical theory) had additional economic costs in terms of wasted output, excess inventories and also in redundant advertising.[10]

Dmitriev's analysis, while presented in a purely theoretical form, was certainly not only of academic relevance. Monopoly was an important element in Russian economy right up until 1913, and arguments in support of monopolistic formations and thus against free competition would have been well received by certain sections of Russian industry and government. The process of industrial concentration had gathered pace in Russia in the last decade of the nineteenth century and the formation of monopolies was a natural concomitant to this. The predominance of large-scale corporation capital, particularly in foreign-owned firms, and the preponderance of government orders encouraged the formation of monopolistic combinations. The elimination of weaker competitors, the syndicated regulation of sales and the setting of monopoly prices were all seen as worthy goals by some sections of Russian industrial leadership.[11] Thus Dmitriev's theoretical support for monopoly in 1904 would have been a welcome tonic to many, although this does not mean that he was simply conjuring theoretically what he thought people wanted to hear.

## The 1891 tariff

Turning away from economic ideas and towards policies, as part of an overall strategy designed to encourage the development of indigenous Russian industry the Minister of Finance, I.A. Vyshnegradsky, set up a working body in 1887 to investigate and design a new tariff structure for goods entering Russian borders. This commission included the world-famous chemist D.I. Mendeleev, who wrote extensive studies of the history of Russian tariff policy and prepared a detailed proposal for the new tariff system. The Russian government had imposed customs duties for many years before 1891, but the previous system was dramatically upgraded and extended in 1891. The justification for the new tariff was three-fold: first fiscal, to generate government revenue; second developmental, to encourage infant industries to grow; and third for protection, to preserve existing manufacturing capacity against the threat of foreign competition. Mendeleev's theoretical support for the 1891 tariff was classical protectionist-style thinking imported directly from Germany and borrowed from Friedrich List, with unfettered free trade being painted as benefiting only advanced countries like Britain.

The results of the tariff are even today controversial, with some Russian industries very likely benefiting but at a definite cost to the domestic consumer. Some have argued that the tariff continued to exist well beyond any time span justified in terms of developing infant industries, while others have suggested that Mendeleev was simply the mouthpiece of specific industrial interests against the interests of the Russian nation as a whole. Tugan-Baranovsky implied that the tariff was partially successful in its aim of encouraging domestic industries, but only because of a previous period of far lower customs protection. Others have suggested that the negative effects of the tariff have been exaggerated in that entrepreneurs overcame the barriers through various skillful manoeuvrings. However the Russian tariff was only one part of a general atmosphere of protection in Europe and America at the end of the nineteenth century and some have suggested that raising tariffs in this isolationist context was indeed a rational strategy, one that did assist industrial growth for those concerned at the time.

## Sergei Witte and industrialisation

A very important figure in Russian economic policy-making at the end of the nineteenth century was Sergei Witte (1849–1915), who was Minister of Finance from 1892 to 1903. Witte's programme for encouraging Russian industrialisation involved a number of interrelated elements of economic policy that were mainly implemented by the state. Monetary stability was achieved by means of introducing the gold standard, tariff protection was raised in order to foster indigenous industry, the level of taxation was increased in order to provide government funds, foreign investment was encouraged so as to foster the use of the most advanced technology, and agricultural exports were stimulated in order to help in maintaining a favourable balance of trade.[12] Many of these elements will be examined in more detail in the sections that follow.

In this programme Witte was (like Mendeleev) in part inspired by the German economist Friedrich List and by protectionist ideas in general, although he was concerned to tailor these ideas to the specific circumstances of Russia. Before his appointment as Minister, Witte had published a long pamphlet on List in which he opined the benefits of national protection, List being touted as the prophet of recent German success. Both List and Witte had extensive practical experience of railway affairs, and in his pamphlet Witte encouraged Russian statesmen to become acquainted with List's works. On achieving office in 1892 Witte embarked upon a policy programme that attempted to adapt List's ideas to Russia, starting with the railways.

## The development of the railways

One key component of Tsarist industrialisation strategy was state assistance to the railways and efforts to greatly extend the railway network in Russia, a component that was by and large successfully accomplished. In the 1890s the Russian state invested directly in the railway infrastructure. When Witte became Minister of Finance in 1892 expenditure on the railways mushroomed from 50 million rubles per year in the six years up to 1892 to 275 million rubles per year from 1893 to 1900.[13] A Trans-Siberian railway was constructed and 25,000 km of new track was laid in the 1890s, which greatly improved the transport system and also assisted in developing new trading networks. The financial policy specialist I.Kh. Ozerov outlined the growth of Russian state expenditure in various government Ministries between 1881 and 1902 as shown in Table 2.1.

The huge growth of expenditure in the Ministry for Transport is the most striking feature of this table, although the budgets of all the other Ministries also grew considerably. Thus the general economic significance of government in Russia increased in the final two decades of the nineteenth century, although it was also important before this time.

*Table 2.1* Ministerial budgets in Russia (in rubles per year)

| Ministry | Year | |
|---|---|---|
| | *1881* | *1902* |
| War | 225,664,000 | 325,639,000 |
| Maritime | 30,467,000 | 98,319,000 |
| Transport | 12,147,000 | 435,548,000 |
| Finance | 108,369,000 | 335,198,000 |

Source: Ozerov, *Ekonomicheskaya Rossiya eya finansovaya politika na iskhod XIX i v nachal XX veka*, p. 237.

## Russian monetary policy 1890–1913

A variant of the gold standard was introduced in Russia in 1897, with notes being convertible into gold on demand at a fixed rate. Witte had been pursuing this policy for some time before 1897, its fundamental aim being to stabilise the ruble and hence boost confidence in the Russian financial system in order to encourage foreign investment in domestic industry. The accumulation of a very large gold reserve in the State Bank was seen as strategically crucial in that only a fully backed convertible currency would generate absolute confidence in the ruble from overseas investors. Some have suggested that such a large holding of gold in bank vaults might have been wasteful, since if it was held overseas it might have generated interest, but this is missing the point about the necessity of boosting confidence in the perceived fragility of the Russian financial system by indigenous means.[14] As Table 2.2 shows, the aim of fully backing issued paper currency by gold had been achieved in Russia by 1913. It would be the ensuing war and the necessity of funding the Allied military campaign that would fatefully render this achievement null and void.

## Russian tax policy and government debt

In the period 1870 to 1913 significant changes occurred in Russian tax policy. A greater reliance on indirect as opposed to direct taxes occurred, together with a shift to some type of progressive system with respect to direct taxes. Whilst in 1870 indirect taxes such as those on alcohol and customs duties made up around 67 per cent of the total, by 1913 they constituted approximately 83 per cent of the total.[15] This favouring of indirect taxation was explained in part by the fact that such taxes were easier to collect and were less burdensome to the wealthy, and partly by the large increase in available consumer goods. Although a graduated income tax was not actually introduced before 1913, tax rates were differentiated by sources and sizes of income based on a judgment of occupational profitability. Even so direct taxes on the very wealthy remained relatively light

*Table 2.2* Gold reserves and currency in circulation in Russia, 1892–1913

| Date | Currency in circulation (millions of rubles) | State bank gold reserves (millions of rubles) | Percentage cover of currency by gold |
|---|---|---|---|
| 1892 | 1055 | 642 | 60.9 |
| 1893 | 1074 | 852 | 79.3 |
| 1894 | 1072 | 895 | 83.5 |
| 1895 | 1048 | 912 | 87.0 |
| 1896 | 1055 | 964 | 91.4 |
| 1897 | 1068 | 1095 | 102.5 |
| 1898 | 901 | 1185 | 131.5 |
| 1899 | 662 | 1008 | 152.3 |
| 1900 | 491 | 843 | 171.7 |
| 1901 | 555 | 735 | 132.4 |
| 1902 | 542 | 710 | 130.9 |
| 1903 | 554 | 769 | 138.8 |
| 1904 | 578 | 909 | 157.3 |
| 1905 | 854 | 1032 | 120.8 |
| 1906 | 1207 | 927 | 76.8 |
| 1907 | 1195 | 1191 | 99.7 |
| 1908 | 1155 | 1169 | 101.2 |
| 1909 | 1087 | 1220 | 112.2 |
| 1910 | 1174 | 1415 | 120.5 |
| 1911 | 1235 | 1451 | 117.5 |
| 1912 | 1327 | 1436 | 108.2 |
| 1913 | 1495 | 1555 | 104.0 |

Sources: Data taken from Finn-Enotaevskii, *Kapitalizm v Rossii, 1890–1917*, p. 247 and p. 254 and Kahan, *Russian Economic History*, p. 104.

up until 1913, the government maintaining inherited privilege in this area as in many others.

Another very important feature of the late imperial economy was the high level of Russian government debt that was held and the amount of resources devoted simply to servicing it. By 1903 the level of government debt had reached approximately 6.6 billion rubles, and over the period 1902–1913 around 13 per cent of national expenditure (approximately 4 billion rubles) went on payments of interest and capital on this debt.[16] If this is added to the cost of war and defence from 1903–1913 (around 9.8 billion rubles), a figure of 13.8 billion or 44.5 per cent of total national expenditure is obtained, indicating the large element of nonproductive expenditure in the late imperial Russian budget, a fact which weighed heavily on ordinary workers and peasants.

## Foreign capital in Russia

A highly charged political question, the extent of foreign ownership of Russian industrial enterprises was much discussed by contemporary economists and also subsequently by historians. However it is difficult to obtain a fully 'neutral' account of this question given that interested parties were often grinding axes of particular types. Moreover the aim of encouraging foreign investment was one element of the industrialisation strategy that was pursued by Witte, and hence those supportive and those critical of this policy came equipped with tailored historical analyses of the importance (or otherwise) of foreign capital to Russian development.

One empirical account of foreign capital – provided by Bovykin in the Soviet period – calculated that total foreign investment in pre-revolutionary Russia (including investment in joint stock companies, state loans and government railway stock) grew from 2662 million rubles in 1881, to 4732 million in 1900, then to 7634 in 1914. By far the largest share was invested in state and railway loans, but the amount invested in joint stock companies increased also from only 3.7 per cent of the total in 1881, to 25.7 per cent of the total in 1914.[17] In terms of the national origin of foreign investment in Russian joint stock companies, Ol' calculated that 33 per cent was French, 23 per cent British, 20 per cent German, 14 per cent from Belgium and 5 per cent from the USA. Each country specialised in certain areas of industrial activity; the British in oil and gold mining for example, the French and the Belgians in mining, metallurgy and banking. In general the importance of foreign capital in Russia was undoubtedly high in the two decades or so before the First World War, Witte explicitly encouraging its prevalence.

## Business cycles in late imperial Russia

A question related to the importance of foreign capital that was much debated by economists in Tsarist Russia was: to what extent did the Russian business cycle follow an independent path or simply mimic the cyclical pattern in the West? This question was in turn connected to the question of whether the Russian economy was becoming integrated into the international (capitalist) economy. Other components of this debate were to what extent indigenous agricultural factors determined the progress of the business cycle and to what extent domestic as against foreign capital drove industrial expansion. As domestic agricultural factors (i.e. the success of the harvest) declined in importance in determining Russian conjuncture, and overseas investments in Russia grew, it might be assumed that Russian cycles would become increasingly harmonised with international movements. On the other hand, as significant levels of indigenous Russian capital began to accumulate, then this might offset some of the increase in international influence.

The Russian economist S.A. Pervushin provided a detailed account of the progress of business cycles in pre-revolutionary Russia. His analysis indicated that the periodicity of fluctuations were as follows: There was an economic upturn at the start of the 1870s that was only short-lived, as from 1872–1876 there was a period of stagnation. A new revival at the end of the 1870s reached a peak in 1878–1879 and was then followed by a depression in 1882–1886. A temporary revival in 1887–1889 was followed by another depression in 1891–1892. An upturn in 1893 led to a period of prosperity that reached its high point in 1899, and this was followed by a crisis in 1900 and then a long depression between 1902–1908. A new upturn from 1909–1913 was observed at the end of this period.[18]

Pervushin also provided an analysis of the relation between various indicators during the business cycle, particularly the relation between the harvest and industrial activity. According to Pervushin the level of the Russian harvest was above average in 1870–1874, 1877–1878, 1881, 1883–1884, 1886–1888, 1893–1896, 1899, 1902, 1904, 1909–1910 and 1912–1913. However, a comparison of this data with cyclical movements failed to reveal a close connection between the two phenomena. Pervushin argued that this was because the harvest in any single year was not the decisive measure, rather harvests from the previous two to three years, the grain price level, and the amount of grain exported had also to be taken into account. Pervushin instead presented a graph showing the level of grain exports against the dividends paid by joint-stock companies, which he suggested clearly demonstrated the link between agricultural changes and the business cycle.[19] Table 2.3 shows Pervushin's overview of cycles for England and Russia between 1870 and 1914.

Russian economists also contributed significantly to the theoretical understanding of business cycles at this time. For example, Tugan-Baranovsky explained industrial crises in the UK by the accumulation and exhaustion of free loanable capital, in tandem with the restricted level of consumption of the working masses and the disproportional development of industrial branches. He also gave a detailed empirical description of cycles, documenting the level of gold bullion in the central bank, the value of exports, the price of iron and the level of bankruptcies. Dmitriev however provided a quite different theory of business cycles to that given by either Pervushin or Tugan-Baranovsky. In Dmitriev's view the increases in labour productivity and falls in production costs brought about by technical progress caused the successive alternation of periods of expansion and contraction. This was because manufacturers worked for the requirements of intermediaries such as wholesale merchants, rather than accumulating stocks themselves or producing directly for consumers. As a consequence of this separation of trading and industrial functions, traders might desire to increase their holdings of stocks in some instances for reasons other than greater consumer demand; to gain the upper hand against competitors for example. For Dmitriev over-production was the result, which led to dramatic price falls and the sudden restriction of output, as the excess goods that were made eventually flooded the market.[20] The works of Tugan-Baranovsky, Pervushin and Dmitriev all had significant influence on Western accounts of cycles such as that developed contemporaneously by Wesley Mitchell, Simon Kuznets and J.M. Keynes.

*Table 2.3* Pervushin's business cycles, 1870–1914

| Year | England | Russia |
|------|---------|--------|
| 1870 | Recovery | Recovery |
| 1871 | Prosperity | Prosperity |
| 1872 | Prosperity | Depression |
| 1873 | Prosperity | Depression |
| 1874 | Crisis | Depression |
| 1875 | Depression | Depression |
| 1876 | Depression | Depression |
| 1877 | Depression | Depression |
| 1878 | Depression | Recovery |
| 1879 | Recovery | Prosperity |
| 1880 | Prosperity | Prosperity |
| 1881 | Prosperity | Depression |
| 1882 | Prosperity | Depression |
| 1883 | Depression | Depression |
| 1884 | Depression | Depression |
| 1885 | Depression | Depression |
| 1886 | Depression | Depression |
| 1887 | Recovery | Recovery |
| 1888 | Recovery | Recovery |
| 1889 | Recovery | Recovery |
| 1890 | Recovery | Depression |
| 1891 | Depression | Depression |
| 1892 | Depression | Depression |
| 1893 | Depression | Recovery |
| 1894 | Depression | Recovery |
| 1895 | Recovery | Recovery |
| 1896 | Recovery | Recovery |
| 1897 | Prosperity | Depression |
| 1898 | Prosperity | Recovery |
| 1899 | Prosperity | Prosperity |
| 1900 | Prosperity | Depression |
| 1901 | Depression | Crisis |
| 1902 | Depression | Depression |
| 1903 | Depression | Recovery |
| 1904 | Recovery | Depression |
| 1905 | Prosperity | Depression |
| 1906 | Prosperity | Depression |
| 1907 | Prosperity | Depression |
| 1908 | Depression | Depression |
| 1909 | Depression | Recovery |
| 1910 | Recovery | Prosperity |
| 1911 | Prosperity | Depression |
| 1912 | Prosperity | Depression |
| 1913 | Depression | Depression |
| 1914 | Depression | Depression |

Source: Pervushin, *Khozyaistvennaya kon'yunktura*, p. 186.

## The institutions of the Tsarist economy

Belief (both genuine and functional) in the divine right of the monarch as absolute ruler was widespread amongst the ruling elite in Tsarist Russia, although this belief was less widespread amongst intellectuals. Consequently the institutions of the Tsarist economy were structured to follow the divine right of the monarch to operate the levers of state power through his ministerial appointments and individual decisions. The system of Russian financial management for example had the Minister of Finance as head, and under the Minister were various departments such as the state treasury, tax revenue, customs revenue, railway affairs and credit. Banks such as the State Savings Bank and the Nobles' and Peasants' Banks were subordinated directly to the Minister, and bureaucratic centralisation characterised the system. The urban bureaucracy distrusted the local self-government institutions to a large degree, and was completely separate from them.[21]

Interpreting 'institutions' in a Veblenian sense, the behavioural habits of Russian peasants, workers and employers were part of Russian culture generally, which was at the time heavily imbued with religious and semi-feudalistic attitudes. As mentioned in the introduction, the importance of the Russian *mir*, or village community, was unquestionable to many. The *mir* was self-sufficient and based on communitarian principles, with assets and obligations being divided equally and with a village assembly to decide on communal affairs. The assembly also dealt with external relations with outside bodies, and within the *mir* agricultural land was periodically re-distributed among members to prevent any inequalities becoming too ingrained. As the large majority of Russian people were peasants, the cultural conventions associated with such institutions as the *mir* were of great importance to understanding indigenous economic habits. Individualistic notions of personal gain through economic exchange were not found extensively within the commune, where collective ties of family and village defined many aspects of peasant life.

One particularly well-known original institution of pre-revolutionary Russia was the *zemstvo*. *Zemstva* were elective agencies composed of representatives from three groups or estates – the peasantry, the gentry and the townsmen. They were charged with conducting purely local governmental functions and they sometimes interacted with other organs such as the ministries. The character of corporate rule by the three estates was nominally one of self-government, although this had been carefully designed not to present a danger to Tsarist rule.[22] Even so the existence of the *zemstvo* demonstrated that agrarian affairs in Russia were managed in quite a different way to those in Western Europe, and attention is now turned to this area in detail.

## The development of agriculture and Stolypin's reforms

There were a number of significant developments in Russian agriculture between 1890 and 1913. The economist P.P. Migulin documented the growth of land ownership among various segments of the rural population between 1893 and 1901 as shown in Table 2.4.

The data presented in this table demonstrated that the price of land increased significantly in a relatively short period – 1897–1898 – as did the quantity of land purchased by the listed categories of buyers. Migulin accounted for the observed rise in price as being a natural part of the general upturn that occurred at this time in the Russian economy, although rising demand as a result of population growth also played its part. The largest purchasers of land by far of the three listed categories were associations (*tovarishchestva*), who usually paid a significantly higher price than did agricultural societies.

A Peasants' Land Bank had been founded in 1882 and a Nobles' Land Bank in 1885, both being part of the State Bank structure, and (as mortgage banks) both assisted in the purchase of land by their respective clientele. In general the land holdings of peasants (both communal and private) increased noticeably between 1861 and 1913, whilst the land holdings of the nobility and the state declined somewhat in this period. Within the peasantry economic differentiation occurred, as had been noted by Lenin, resulting in the creation of a layer of market-based producers who sold only or mainly for profit, yielding a concomitant rise in the marketability of many foodstuffs.

Perhaps the single most important development in agriculture between 1890 and 1913 was the reforms undertaken by Peter Stolypin to encourage private ownership of farms and to create a significant class of enterprising

*Table* 2.4  The quantity and price of land purchased

| Year | The quantity of land purchased by: (in desyatins) | | | The price of land purchased by: (in rubles per desyatin) | | |
|------|------------------------|--------------|------------------------|------------------------|--------------|------------------------|
| | Agricultural societies | Associations | Individual citizens | Agricultural societies | Associations | Individual citizens |
| 1893 | 37,990  | 113,925 | 5,383  | 33 | 56 | 55  |
| 1894 | 38,800  | 136,954 | 5,211  | 32 | 54 | 45  |
| 1895 | 23,008  | 152,623 | 7,611  | 35 | 55 | 42  |
| 1896 | 44,416  | 156,036 | 6,207  | 38 | 52 | 56  |
| 1897 | 90,735  | 259,054 | 6,525  | 56 | 77 | 69  |
| 1898 | 167,442 | 410,813 | 11,974 | 70 | 78 | 86  |
| 1899 | 157,282 | 541,902 | 18,202 | 72 | 79 | 77  |
| 1900 | 135,592 | 660,809 | 20,964 | 82 | 82 | 90  |
| 1901 | 97,564  | 660,622 | 16,065 | 88 | 91 | 130 |

Source: Migulin, *Nasha bankovaya politika*, pp. 395–6.

peasant landowners. In November 1906 Stolypin introduced land reform legislation to enable peasants to break away from the commune and form their own private holdings with their share of the communal land, which would not be divided into strips but would be farmed as a unified parcel. The actual process of separation was, however, lengthy and far from simple, and the response from peasants was moderate at best. By 1915 around 10 per cent of peasant households had created independent farms, but only approximately 25 per cent of these farms had actually fully departed from the village.[23] Even so, given that Stolypin had wanted twenty years or so for this policy to be completed and that it was actually interrupted after only nine years – by the First World War – it cannot be counted as a total failure or dismissed as completely ineffective.

Stolypin's land reforms were discussed in detail by various economists of the day. For example in a pamphlet focusing solely on the decree of 9 November 1906, A.I. Chuprov suggested that the agricultural improvements required could be accomplished without breaking the existing communal order.[24] He characterised the decree as a harsh challenge to the Russian people that destroyed the long-term order of agricultural relations, suggesting that he was not at all in favour of it.[25] Other economists such as N.P. Oganovsky argued that granting peasants the right of private property would reinforce their separateness and their sense of isolation from the rest of society. In 1917 Kondratiev believed that Stolypin had been wrong to attempt to eradicate the commune by force, the Socialist Revolutionary Kondratiev being politically to the left of Stolypin at this time. Government officials had placed some significant pressure on peasants to leave the commune, in retrospect this most likely being what Kondratiev objected to.

Another significant development in post-1900 Russian agriculture was the growing importance of cooperatives. By 1914 17,000 agricultural cooperatives with a membership of eight or nine million people were in existence, the cooperative movement encompassing around one quarter of all peasant households by this time. Witte had supported the development of cooperatives in 1904, viewing them as antithetical to the peasant commune. The commune was seen as primitive and based on undifferentiated collective ownership, whereas the cooperative was viewed as dynamic, uniting individuals (rather than family units) and fostering initiative.[26] Moreover in cooperatives members were selected by occupation and function, and were often required to purchase shares on joining. Government encouragement of cooperatives took the form of enabling cooperative credit in a statute issued in 1904 and providing additional funds and personnel from 1910 onwards. In general agricultural cooperation was indeed institutionally distinct from the peasant commune, but a similar spirit of communal responsibility was found in its *modus operandi*, as witnessed, for example, in the notion of collective responsibility for all debts. Even so Lenin would act to nationalise cooperatives in 1918.

## The war with Japan and the 1905 revolution

In the decade or so before the First World War, political events continued to impress themselves forcefully upon the developing Russian economy. In January 1904 Japan attacked the Russian fleet at Port Arthur as a consequence of disagreements over Russia's leasing of a Chinese peninsula and the subsequent occupation of Manchuria. The course of the war was characterised by a series of painful defeats for Russia and Japanese victory came in autumn 1905. The war with Japan provided a rallying point for opponents of Tsarism, and in 1905 a mass movement in favour of a Constituent Assembly elected on the basis of universal suffrage broke out, together with calls for freedom of speech and limitations to the working day. Following a successful general strike, a politically radical Council of Workers' Deputies was formed in St Petersburg containing Mensheviks, Bolsheviks and Socialist Revolutionaries. As a consequence of these events the Tsar responded with a series of concessions including the formation of an elected body (the Duma) and granting the right of free citizenship to all.

In terms of economic consequences, the war with Japan left a legacy in Russian ruling circles of believing that Russia needed urgently to improve its system of supply of weapons and military equipment, a key weakness identified in the Japanese campaign. The financial cost of the war had been significant, and had been covered to a large extent by increased borrowing and also by the issuing of notes. The revolutionary events of 1905 compounded the financial crisis that had been provoked by the war, and increased strain was placed on the gold standard system as concerned citizens demanded gold and the level of savings held in Russian banks declined. To help in solving this crisis Minister of Finance Kokovtsov negotiated a new French loan in April 1906, although the further necessity of cuts in planned budget expenditure followed throughout 1906.[27]

However, by 1912 Russia was committed to an ambitious programme of naval rearmament, in part conditioned by international factors but also encouraged by the reappearance of Imperial pretensions on the domestic front. Russia had signed up to a new diplomatic consensus with France and Britain, which had serious consequences with respects to the Russian armaments industries in particular and the Russian economy in general. Economics is not always war by other means, but war certainly has implications for economic development.

## V.N. Kokovtsov as Minister of Finance

In important element of the design of post-war economic policy fell to the Minister of Finance of the time, V.N. Kokovtsov. Kokovtsov's own analysis of his period in office is worth considering in detail. He claimed that he blazed no new trails for the economic progress of Russia, rather he endeavoured merely to preserve what was already in existence. The basic

principle that underlay all his financial policy decisions was said to be balanced budgets through fiscal conservatism, i.e. that ordinary state expenditure should be covered by ordinary state revenue. Any projected increase
in expenditure should be covered by natural increases in revenue accruing
from the development of the nation's productive forces, increases in taxation being allowed only as a secondary measure or to fund unforeseen
extraordinary expenditure. He also believed that private enterprise best
accomplished the development of the productive forces in Russia, although
state enterprise should certainly coexist with private whilst being restricted
to certain specific fields of activity.

Kokovtsov's first period as Minister of Finance – from 1904 to the
middle of 1907 – was dominated by the war with Japan, which he
attempted to finance by negotiating a new loan rather than by raising
taxes. His second period as Minister – from the middle of 1907 to the
beginning of 1914 – was characterised by measures directed towards stimulating economic recovery and reconstruction.[28] In the first period the
financial situation became at times very precarious, with Kokovtsov
actively considering whether to discontinue the free exchange of gold for
currency.[29] The loan eventually provided by France to assist in the war was
approximately 620.2 million rubles, a quite significant sum at the time.[30]
According to some commentators the fate of the Russian monarchy itself
lay entirely in the hands of the high financiers of the French money market
at this crucial moment.[31]

In his second period as Minister Kokovtsov tried concertedly to pay off
the loan negotiated to finance the Japanese campaign, and he did successfully balance the state budget in the years from 1910 to 1913 inclusive. In
terms of progressive reforms he made the necessary financial appropria-
tions in order to introduce general education into the country by 1920, set
aside large sums for improvements in agriculture such as distributing fer-
tilisers and agricultural machinery, and took steps to make credit available
to the lower classes through municipalities and *zemstvo* institutions. Such
plans for improvements were however disrupted by the outbreak of war in
1914.

In relation to a sectoral breakdown of government expenditure, under
Kokovtsov's tutelage total ordinary state expenditure grew from 1883
million rubles in 1904 to 3070 million in 1913, an increase of approximately 63 per cent. However within this total figure, expenditure on cultural and productive projects increased the most in percentage terms, from
213.7 million rubles to 519.2 million or by 143 per cent, whilst expenditure on administration grew by only 54 per cent, on national defence by
75 per cent and on state enterprise by 41 per cent.[32] Hence the charge
sometimes levied that the Russian government of the period was more
willing to spend on defence or administration rather than the cultural
needs of the country was, according to Kokovtsov, inaccurate, especially
when it was acknowledged that some expenditure classified as non-cultural

was actually cultural. However, despite Kokovtsov's protestations, state expenditure on cultural and productive projects was still significantly less in 1913 than expenditure on defence or on state enterprises when measured in absolute terms.

Kokovtsov explained that he was able to achieve the various increases in state expenditure without any large increase in taxation or without the introduction of many new taxes, because of the steadily increasing revenue provided by the development of Russia's productive forces. The level of per capita taxation paid by the Russian people grew only marginally in the period under review, from 10.31 rubles in 1908 to 10.84 rubles in 1912. It was even possible to accumulate a surplus of 518 million rubles by the time of the start of the First World War.[33] In terms of overall economic growth Kokovtsov outlined that the volume of Russian foreign trade increased significantly from 1682 million rubles in 1904 to 2690 million in 1913, the total amount of money held in Russian financial institutions grew from 11,300 million rubles in 1904 to 19,000 million rubles in 1913, the level of cast iron produced increased from 2490 million kilograms in 1903 to 4636 million in 1913, and the amount of coal that was mined grew from 17,871 million kilograms in 1903 to 36,265 million in 1913.[34] Consequently it was from such specific levels of growth that Kokovtsov was able to increase total state revenue to the amount indicated by 1913. In general Kokovtsov's efforts as Minister of Finance can be judged as well intentioned, but perhaps insufficiently radical or far-reaching to be able to tackle Russia's underlying problems at source, given that major structural reforms were not attempted.

## Innovative entrepreneurs or robber barons?

The development of certain branches of Russian industry was closely connected to the activities of various foreign and indigenous business magnates who became inextricably associated with the particular industrial branch in question. For example the name of the German industrialist Ludwig Knoop was linked to the introduction of mechanical cotton spinning in Russia, in the end controlling 122 cotton factories. The Welshman John Hughes helped to create an iron industry in the Ukraine, eventually having a town named after him. The Swedish Nobel company was responsible for developing much of Russia's oil industry. Of indigenous industrialists the Gukhov family and the Konovalov family were famous as merchant entrepreneurs, the Gukhov's controlling textile factories. But how was the activities of these magnates viewed by Russian economists of the time, were they seen as extremely valuable assets essential to further industrial development, or parasitical tycoons who drained the real producers of their just rewards? A mixture of both attitudes was very likely present, as will been seen in what follows.

Tugan-Baranovsky for example called Knoop the undisputed lord of the weaving industry and suggested that his role in modernising a crude and sluggish Russian capitalism was genuinely outstanding. Knoop's business interests built virtually all of the cotton mills in the central industrial region of Russia. However, Knoop had come to Russia after first spending a year in Manchester and he began as an importer of cotton and yarn, subsequently moving on to manufacturing equipment.[35] According to one source Knoop's method (after he was firmly established) was that a manufacturer who desired a factory was obliged to call at Knoop's office and make an application. If this was successful detailed plans of the factory would be then sent from England, and then when construction was complete, machinery would follow along the same route as the plans. Knoop succeeded first and foremost by 'dexterous financial and diplomatic management' and one author even referred to 'men like Rockefeller and Knoop'.[36]

However, foreign entrepreneurs did not build all of Russian industry before 1917. Gerschenkron emphasised the importance of indigenous old-believer entrepreneurs to the beginnings of industrial growth in Russia from the 1840s onwards. Old believers were a conservative movement who had refused to part with ancient religious customs. Organised groups of old believers participated in economic development through charitable activities, mutual aid and conventional business activity, their motivation stemming from their position as a social group and their desire for economic advancement.[37] This suggests that Russian entrepreneurial development occurred as the result of a complex mixture of both domestic and overseas influences.

In general it is useful in the Russian context to distinguish between entrepreneurs and capitalists, the former undertaking the manufacturing risk associated with the innovation of a new product or productive technique, the latter assuming only the financial risk of new investment. The two activities were often quite different, with distinct motivations and outcomes.[38] It was the entrepreneur who was more likely to be the real innovator, the capitalist simply following the opportunity for profit. Successful entrepreneurs could become capitalists, but it was rare that capitalists became entrepreneurs. In the Russian case some capitalists were certainly of domestic origin, but overseas personnel more usually fulfilled the entrepreneurial function, i.e. product innovation came for example from the UK. This might be seen to have serious consequences, in that if this characterisation was even partially applicable, Russia was indigenous entrepreneur-deficient but did not lack capitalists to the same extent. On the other hand it could be suggested that insufficient time had elapsed by 1913 for Russian entrepreneurship to develop its full potential, or that in Russia the distinction between capitalist and entrepreneur was less applicable. The opposite number of the business magnate was the ordinary factory worker, to which attention is now turned.

## Labour conditions

There were around two million industrial workers in Russia in 1897, and by 1913 this number had risen to approximately three million. This was a relatively small figure in relation to the overall population, but the Russian proletariat lived in concentrated urban locations that gave it dis-proportional political significance. In terms of the conditions of the working class in Russia, who provided the labour employed by the industrial magnates, various evaluations have been provided. One visitor to Russia in June 1888, a British Consul-General, reported unfavourably that factory workers were generally housed in dwellings unfit for human habitation, only rarely being provided with access to hospitals and schools, and had their wages cut for the slightest irregularity in performance. This had caused the outbreak of many strikes that were often suppressed by the police.[39] In general labour conditions in pre-revolutionary Russia were indeed poor, with long hours worked for low pay and with poor safety provisions.

Various legal reforms occurred in the 1880s and 1890s in relation to the employment conditions of women and children, such as those implemented in June 1882, June 1885 and April 1890. For example the law of June 1882 set a lower limit for employment at the age of 12, and regulated the working hours of children between the ages of 12 and 15, limiting them to eight or nine hours per day.[40] The law of June 1885 prohibited night work for persons below 17 years of age. Overall, three aspects of labour legislation can be identified as being important at this time. Laws relating to the working hours of women and children, as identified previously, laws regulating the hiring of labour and the relation between owner and worker (June 1886 and June 1903), and laws relating to protecting injured workers (June 1903). However some manufacturers were opposed to these new measures and accused the Minister responsible – N.Kh. Bunge – of failing to understand Russian conditions. This suggests that concern for the well-being of workers was not always uppermost in the minds of Russian business magnates.

## M.I. Tugan-Baranovsky and the Russian factory

Depending on the point of view adopted, business magnates and their employed workers either collided or cooperated in the factory environment. M.I. Tugan-Baranovsky (1865–1919) was undoubtedly one of the most profound economic thinkers that Tsarist Russia ever produced, and his reputation is (in part) built upon his major work in economic history, *The Russian Factory in the Past and the Present*. In the preface to this work Tugan-Baranovsky explained that a basic aim was to trace how the original merchant-owned factory was transformed into the gentry-owned factory, which then became the modern capitalist factory.[41] The impression conveyed was of an organic series of transformations in which the continuities were as important as the fractures. Moreover various important themes reoccurred throughout *The Russian Factory* (and in Tugan-Baranovsky's work in general), eight of the most important being:

1   The simplistic opposition of state against private forms of economy with regards to Russian industrial development was a misnomer.
2   The Russian economy was without doubt becoming part of the world economy.
3   Support for small-scale rural forms of economy was a dead-end.
4   The import of foreign capital was crucial to Russian economic development.
5   The growth of capitalism in Russia could in no way be hindered by a lack of overseas markets for Russian goods.
6   The idea of a linear scheme of industrial transformation, for example the replacement of small-scale *kustar* (handicraft) production with the large capitalist factory, was an oversimplification.
7   The absence of the city in its West European form had important consequences for the form of capital prevalent in Russia.
8   Russian industrial fluctuations were being caused by the periodic creation of free loanable capital.

Some of these themes have been touched upon earlier in this chapter, others will be expanded upon in what follows.

Regarding theme one, for Tugan-Baranovsky the role of the state was to enable and encourage private industry and not necessarily to replace it. This became clearer in his analysis of exactly how Peter the Great had fostered large-scale industry in Russia. The large-scale production that was established during Peter's reign was based on the (private) commercial capital that had been built-up 'naturally' in pre-Petrine Russia. The great majority of the factory owners of the Petrine period were Russian merchants. Hence large-scale industry was in fact created in Russia by Petrine support for such industry, *in combination with* the commercial milieu of the great merchants that was the result of the preceding 'natural' history of the Muscovite state.[42] Moreover while those factories deemed especially necessary – mines, munitions and textiles – had initially been set up by the government, they were then transferred to private control. The government had provided interest-free loans to entrepreneurs who were establishing factories, and even given all this the overwhelming majority of Petrine factories had been created privately, without state assistance. Hence the simplistic opposition of state to private forms of economy was misleading.

Regarding theme six, it was Tugan-Baranovsky's view that large-scale industrial capital not only did not oppress and destroy small-scale industry, but in fact actually assisted in its development in the pre-reform period. In contrast to the widespread conception of the folk origins of handicraft manufacture, sometimes it was the factory that gave birth to cottage industry and not *vice versa*. For example handicraft cotton printing sprang up as a result of the large cotton factories created at the end of the eighteenth century, and even contributed to the eventual dissolution of such large factories. The introduction of new types of machinery had led to the factory prevailing over handicrafts in certain branches such as cotton weaving, because handicraft manufacture could not compete. However, this process simultaneously led to the founding of new branches of handicrafts production in areas such as sheepskin-coat manufacture and some metal trades.[43] Tugan-Baranovsky stressed that, against the romantic view of cottage industry propagated by some, in fact it was a 'typical form of the so-called sweating system with all its horrors'.[44]

Regarding theme seven, one very significant element in the industrialisation equation was the economic importance of the city. In his *Foundations of Political Economy* Tugan-Baranovsky had stated that the most important difference between the conditions of economic development in Russia and those in Western Europe was the absence in the former of the stage of municipal or urban economy. In Russian history there was no city in the same sense as there was in the Middle Ages in Western Europe; in Russia the city was so small that it 'drowned in the mass of the countryside'. Moreover those cities that had existed had a very different character to those in the West. Western cities were centres of small industry, such industry working not for trading intermediaries but directly for consumers. In Russia, cities were mainly administrative and trading centres, industry being dispersed throughout the countryside.[45]

Because of this fact there was an essential difference between West European urban artisans and Russian rural handicraft workers. The former worked for local inhabitants whereas the latter worked for distant markets, thus necessitating the existence of trading intermediaries. The political predominance of Moscow was thus based on the fact that it was a trading centre for a huge district, the industry of which found itself in direct submission to trading capital. The class that controlled this capital was, after the landed nobility, the most influential class, whilst the class that had played a large role in Western Europe – free urban artisans – was absent. Thus Russia did not possess the organisations of small industrialists on which Western civilisation had arisen.[46]

Regarding Tugan-Baranovsky's view of how industrialisation could best be further promoted in Russia in the future, he could be interpreted as advocating state-assisted market-based industrialisation, in contrast to the state-led bureaucrat-controlled industrialisation eventually attempted by Stalin. Tugan-Baranovsky rejected the idea that capitalist industrialisation was either state-led or market-led; it was this false dualism which much of his work in economic history was directed against. Even so, and in tune with his socialist sympathies, the exploitative nature of much of capitalist industry was certainly not denied.

## Tugan-Baranovsky's view of the late imperial economy

In what follows an exposition of Tugan-Baranovsky's analysis of the Russian economy after 1900 is provided as a contemporaneous summary of developments in the Tsarist period. Tugan-Baranovsky outlined that by the end of the nineteenth century Russian industry had achieved its first major successes. For example in 1886 Russia smelted 532 million kilograms of iron, less than 3 per cent of the world total, but by 1899 this had risen to 2706 million kilograms of iron or 7 per cent of the world total. This had occurred as a direct consequence of Sergei Witte's policies. The introduction of a gold-backed currency had facilitated an inflow of foreign capital, which together with increased railway construction had created the boom of the 1890s.[47] However the upturn of the 1890s had come to a catastrophic end in the autumn of 1899. The 23 September saw a 'black day' on the St Petersburg exchange, with a general crash followed by mass bankruptcy. By the end of 1899 an atmosphere of crisis prevailed in all industrial branches, although it was especially deep in iron production, coal and mining.[48]

Providing an explanation of the unusual persistence of this period of stagnation Tugan-Baranovsky stressed that the Russian crisis differed from the usual periodic fluctuations experienced by capitalist industry. While it was usually the case that the recovery was brought about by the crisis itself, in Russia this appeared not to be happening. The reason why the 1899 crisis had not given way to a new upturn was that Russia was heavily capital-deficient. Indigenous Russian capital accumulated in such insignificant quantities that it could not generate an upturn by itself. The upturn of the 1890s had been possible only because a huge amount of foreign capital had poured into Russia, including 400 million Belgian francs, 15 million pounds and large amounts of German and French funds. Were foreign capitalists likely to invest in Russian enterprises when even the meagre amount of indigenous capital that was in existence was fleeing overseas as a consequence of revolution?[49] Tugan-Baranovsky was suggesting that foreign capitalists had been frightened by political unrest and by the 1904–1905 war with Japan.

However, 1910 did mark a turning point for Russian conjuncture. The decreased danger of new revolutionary outbreaks had created an atmosphere more conducive to capitalist investment, and the prolonged depression had allowed the level of domestic free capital to grow significantly. This can be seen from the data on the deposits and current accounts of joint-stock and savings banks shown in Table 2.5.

This table shows that savings in joint-stock banks almost doubled between January 1907 and April 1910, the level of new free capital assembled in joint-stock and savings banks in this period being over 800 million rubles. Joint-stock banks provided long-term credit to Russian industry for the acquisition of fixed capital, for either the creation of new businesses or the reconstruction of old ones.[50]

*Table 2.5* The level of deposits and current accounts in joint-stock and savings banks

| Date | Joint-stock banks | Date | Savings banks |
|------|-------------------|------|---------------|
| 1 January 1907 | 760.9 | 1 August 1907 | 1089.5 |
| 1 January 1908 | 818.0 | 1 August 1908 | 1164.9 |
| 1 January 1909 | 976.4 | 1 August 1909 | 1216.3 |
| 1 January 1910 | 1262.1 | 1 August 1910 | 1325.3 |
| 1 April 1910 | 1401.6 | – | – |

Source: Tugan-Baranovsky, 'Sostoyanie nashei promyshlennosti za desyatiletie 1900–1909 gg.', p. 507.

Tugan-Baranovsky continued his analysis by relating that Russian imports in the first half of 1910 had increased greatly, in particular the import of means of production. This revival was especially strong in those industrial branches that had suffered the most in the previous depression such as iron production. The price of iron had risen significantly and imports of iron had begun to grow. Shares in railway and machinery companies had also risen dramatically, the underlying cause of this revival being the accumulation of free capital. In conclusion Tugan-Baranovsky predicted that the new upturn would be an important stimulus to the workers movement, to the professional classes and to urban cooperation.[51]

In this article Tugan-Baranovsky at one point stated that a new upturn was impossible without overseas capital, but at another he implied that sufficient free capital had accumulated within Russia to generate a new upturn. According to one source foreign capital as a percentage of total new industrial investment increased from 37 per cent in 1906–1908 to 50 per cent in 1909–1913, suggesting that capital from overseas did play an important role in the upturn that occurred after 1910.[52] Another possibility was that the depression of the 1900s was so prolonged that, for the first time, indigenous Russian capital had accumulated in sufficient amounts to launch a new upturn by itself. That Tugan-Baranovsky was indeed moving towards this explanation can be seen in the next section.

## The Russian economy in 1913

Tugan-Baranovsky began his analysis of the Russian economy on the eve of the First World War by relating that the bad harvest of 1911 had not only failed to provoked an industrial crisis, but did not have much influence on the course of the upturn at all. This was because it had begun as a consequence of the accumulation of significant amounts of free capital on the money markets over previous years. He had predicted that the forthcoming year (1913) would still be successful for industry, but that the rate of growth would slacken.[53] The most important difference was that while the upturn of the 1890s arose wholly on the basis of an inflow of foreign capital from overseas, the current upturn was based on capital accumulation within Russia.[54] This can be seen from an account of the increase of deposits and current accounts in Russian credit institutions and savings banks between 1908 and 1913 given in Table 2.6. Thus between 1908 and 1913 over 2 billion rubles of new prospective capital was deposited, which according to Tugan-Baranovsky had facilitated the significant industrial upturn witnessed in this period.[55]

As a comparison, Lyashchenko related that the concentration of production and an increase in the productivity of enterprises had been actively promoted by the 1900s depression.[56] For Gerschenkron the character of the 1908–1913 boom was fundamentally different to that of the 1890s, as Russian industry had reached a stage when it could dispense with government support and develop independently.[57] Others have disputed this suggestion, pointing to the large increase in defence expenditure by the state after 1908.[58] Tugan's view was that the accumulation of significant indigenous free capital was the most important distinguishing feature comparing the 1908–1913 boom with that of the 1890s. This would signify that Russia had finally made the most important step in becoming a capitalist economy of the West European type.

Turning to the future, for Tugan-Baranovsky some disturbing symptoms were appearing on the economic horizon in 1913. While Russian conjuncture had remained favourable, the West had been standing on the brink of abnormal conditions for more than six months. Indeed the progress of the industrial cycle had recently been rather unusual. European money markets had been shaken at the end of 1911 by the dangers of war, and the costs of mobilisation had created a shortage of free capital that resulted in unprecedented heights in the interest rate. Thus at a time when the industrial upturn was only beginning to develop, the money markets stood at a point usually seen in times of industrial crises. This constrained position of money markets was caused not by the natural processes through which free capital was exhausted, but by political events which were in no way connected to industrial cycles.[59]

Russian conjuncture was still in its ascending phase due to the fact that the upturn had followed a prolonged depression of an unprecedented

*Table 2.6* The level of deposits and current accounts in credit institutions and savings banks

| Year | Credit institutions and savings banks |
| --- | --- |
| 1908 | 2969 |
| 1909 | 3247 |
| 1910 | 3833 |
| 1911 | 4404 |
| 1912 | 4842 |
| 1913 | 5228 |

Source: Tugan-Baranovsky, 'Narodnoe khozyaistvo', p. 349.

nature. However without an influx of foreign capital Tugan-Baranovsky thought that the continuation of the current Russian upturn was unthinkable. For example he suggested that it would be necessary for Russia to borrow an additional 900 million rubles from the West in order to complete the new railway network programme.[60] Tugan-Baranovsky warned that the danger of insufficient free capital was the most serious threat to the continuation of the Russian upturn. This was why Russian bourses had been in a depressed condition for months. In 1914 Tugan-Baranovsky predicted a crisis and an industrial depression to follow.[61]

Gerschenkron provided an apt summary of developments in the Russian economy over the period 1906–1914. Industrial growth had resumed after the depression of the early 1900s and a withdrawal of the state from the industrialisation process had occurred. Banks had emerged as a leading source of capital investment, improvements in the position of workers had occurred together with a reduction in the financial burden imposed on the peasantry.[62] For Gerschenkron this indicated that Witte's policies pursued in the 1890s had finally proved their worth, whereas Tugan-Baranovsky was more pessimistic about the prospects for continued growth after 1913. Others have highlighted various factors enabling the general transformation of Russian industry in the last quarter of the nineteenth century. For example the emancipation of the peasants, the abolition of taxation by mutual guarantee (which held the peasants to the village), the promotion of learning by *zemstvo* authorities and the subsequent education of workers, and the attraction of Russia to foreign capital have all been listed.[63] Overall one of the most serious hindrance to further progress was not any narrowly economic factor, but the outmoded political system in which the Russian economy had still to function.

## Conclusion

On the eve of the First World War Russian industry was developing significantly, if unevenly, and Russian economics had shown itself to be a vital discipline containing a number of competing currents that generally coexisted, if at times a little uneasily. This pre-war pluralism did not always influence government policy decisions however, which followed a more narrow gauge of opinion, rather than being completely open to any and all suggestion. Witte's industrialisation strategy had been rather successful, Stolypin's agricultural reforms a little less so. Whether Russian industry could have continued to develop successfully after 1913 without significant additional foreign investment was a point of much debate, which would however soon turn out to be purely academic. Most of these developments would be torn asunder by war and revolution, although (as is always the case) the legacy of those recently deceased would continue to weigh heavily on the minds and experiences of the living.

# 3   Revolutionary economy, 1914–1921

## The general impact of the First World War

The First World War proved a violent catalyst for many revolutionary changes in the Western world, including the Bolshevik assumption of power in October 1917. It signalled the end of the *belle époque* and the first beginnings of mass democracy; the finish of the haphazard rule of age-old elites and the stirrings of various participatory movements across Europe and America; the end of the long nineteenth century and the start of the angular modernist configuration. Various causes have been touted as the origins of the war, some of which will be discussed in what follows, but the overall impact of the war as the first large-scale international territorial conflict is difficult to exaggerate.

The battlefield mechanics of trench warfare that were pioneered in Europe between 1914 and 1918 proved to be very bloody and protracted, with random piles of mutilated corpses left mouldering in the mud. But from these haunted corpses a new hope would apparently emerge, as a fatal blow was struck to the Imperial Russian class structure by socialist forces in the autumn of 1917, and the creation of an avowedly communitarian society to replace capitalist production began to occur. Some might argue that the revolutionaries eventually proved gossamer-thin on new economic ideas, others might suggest that the context itself eventually proved insurmountable. To what extent the circumstances of war played a role in significantly handicapping the initial Bolshevik effort is an important question that will be analysed forthwith, together with an account of some of the relevant work produced by economists of the period, and an evaluation of the first steps of the Bolshevik government with respect to creating new socialist economic formations.

## The economic consequences of the war for Russia

Economic policies pursued during the war had important significance for the situation in which the Bolsheviks found themselves in 1917. In order to finance the war and as part of an alliance with the UK and France, Russia had abandoned its proud *idée-fix*, the gold standard, and had resorted to printing vast amounts of paper currency and also to exporting significant levels of gold overseas. The latter occurred at the persistent request of the UK financial authorities and J.M. Keynes himself. The exact amounts of money printed and gold exported during the war are shown in Table 3.1.

This table shows that the percentage cover of currency by gold in Russia declined from 104 per cent in July 1914 to 6.1 per cent in October 1917; a very significant change. This produced an atmosphere of monetary instability that persisted long after the October revolution and that had important consequences for financial planning in the post-war period. In his *Economic Consequences of the Peace* of 1919, Keynes had warned of the potential dangers of excessive reparations, and in his *Tract on Monetary Reform* of 1923, he reported the attainment of a 'sort-of' monetary equilibrium in Russia only by the end of 1922. This followed the final phase of hyperinflation, when the use of legal-tender money had virtually been discarded, which occurred approximately five years after the Bolsheviks had taken power.[1] This was a very long time to live with extreme monetary uncertainty, a period which undoubtedly had long-term consequences for the Bolshevik attempt at creating socialist economy. On the other hand, given that some Bolsheviks had initially welcomed monetary chaos as symbolising the death knell of capitalist production, they could not then consistently blame it for all the shortcomings that were identified in the policies that followed.

In general much Russian industry had been reoriented to the war effort. War Industries Committees were created in May 1915 to mobilise Russian business activity in the required direction, and two well-known industrial magnates – A.I. Gukhov and A.I. Konovalov – were elected to the central committee of one of them. The militarisation of industry affected many sectors of the economy such as metallurgy, chemicals, garments and shoes, which were quickly adapted to the requirements of war. Massive disruption occurred in transportation, agriculture, finance and credit, disturbances that would have serious consequences for post-war reconstruction. In one estimate, the war effort came to occupy 60–70 per cent of all industrial production in Russia, with structural shifts occurring in many sectors of the economy such as the transformation from agricultural machinery to armaments.[2] Whatever the precise causes of war were said to be, its disruptive consequences were beyond dispute.

Whilst the picture rightly painted of the Russian economy during the war is often one of extreme stress and disruption, it is possible to exaggerate this element of the industrial equation, at least with respect to the internal efficiency of enterprises. For example a British Colonel toured 20 private factories in the south of Russia over three weeks in July 1917 – plants such as automobile and aeroplane works, iron and steel works, coal mines and power stations – factories that he believed (perhaps naively) were representative of the conditions found in non-governmental factories throughout Russia.

*Table 3.1* Currency emission and gold reserves in Russia, July 1914 to October 1917

| Date | Currency in circulation (billions of rubles) | Gold reserves (billions of rubles) | Percentage cover of currency by gold |
|------|------|------|------|
| July 1914 | 1.630 | 1.695 | 104.0 |
| August 1914 | 2.321 | 1.695 | 73.0 |
| September 1914 | 2.554 | 1.695 | 66.4 |
| October 1914 | 2.697 | 1.695 | 62.8 |
| November 1914 | 2.791 | 1.620 | 58.0 |
| December 1914 | 2.846 | 1.620 | 56.9 |
| January 1915 | 2.947 | 1.620 | 55.0 |
| February 1915 | 3.059 | 1.620 | 53.0 |
| March 1915 | 3.151 | 1.620 | 51.4 |
| April 1915 | 3.313 | 1.620 | 48.9 |
| May 1915 | 3.362 | 1.620 | 48.2 |
| June 1915 | 3.477 | 1.620 | 46.6 |
| July 1915 | 3.756 | 1.620 | 43.1 |
| August 1915 | 3.962 | 1.620 | 40.9 |
| September 1915 | 4.211 | 1.620 | 38.5 |
| October 1915 | 4.893 | 1.620 | 33.1 |
| November 1915 | 5.041 | 1.620 | 32.1 |
| December 1915 | 5.201 | 1.526 | 29.3 |
| January 1916 | 5.617 | 1.526 | 27.2 |
| February 1916 | 5.709 | 1.526 | 26.7 |
| March 1916 | 5.899 | 1.526 | 25.9 |
| April 1916 | 6.078 | 1.526 | 25.1 |
| May 1916 | 6.213 | 1.526 | 24.6 |
| June 1916 | 6.380 | 1.432 | 22.4 |
| July 1916 | 6.628 | 1.432 | 21.6 |
| August 1916 | 6.876 | 1.432 | 20.8 |
| September 1916 | 7.122 | 1.432 | 20.1 |
| October 1916 | 7.587 | 1.432 | 18.9 |
| November 1916 | 8.083 | 1.244 | 15.4 |
| December 1916 | 8.383 | 1.244 | 14.8 |
| January 1917 | 9.097 | 1.244 | 13.7 |
| February 1917 | 9.440 | 1.056 | 11.2 |
| March 1917 | 9.950 | 1.056 | 10.6 |
| April 1917 | 10.981 | 1.056 | 9.6 |
| May 1917 | 11.457 | 1.056 | 9.2 |
| June 1917 | 12.186 | 1.056 | 8.7 |
| July 1917 | 13.055 | 1.056 | 8.1 |
| August 1917 | 14.125 | 1.056 | 7.5 |
| September 1917 | 15.398 | 1.056 | 6.9 |
| October 1917 | 17.290 | 1.051 | 6.1 |

Source: Column 2 – Katzenellenbaum, *Russian Currency and Banking*, pp. 56–7; Column 3 – Smele, 'White Gold: The Imperial Russian Gold Reserve in the Anti-Bolshevik East', p. 1319, Table 1.

The Colonel reported that he found the layout and working conditions of factories good, or at least equal in this respect to some of the more modern works in England. The volume of work completed was found to be unsatisfactory but he was agreeably surprised by the standard of work and by the general capabilities of the workforce. The machine hands were evaluated as working as efficiently as the average machine hand in England, although skilled workers were not quite up to English standards.[3] Serious flaws were however detected in the system of distribution of raw materials. The Colonel concluded that:

> All the evidence pointed to Russia being eventually able to support herself in practically all branches of manufacture that I saw, with the principal exception of wire for ropes and for aeroplanes ... On the whole the theoretical organisation and the technique of manufacture are fairly good, but there is much to be desired in their application.[4]

Whilst it is quite possible that the Colonel was receiving from his hosts a deliberately rosy picture of the state of Russian industry, it is unlikely that all his favourable observations were wildly inaccurate.

## Internal trade during the war

A key issue for the Russian economy during the First World War was the supply, collection and distribution of food stocks, grain in particular. In terms of supply a bumper harvest in 1913 was followed by an average harvest in 1914 and a somewhat better harvest in 1915, but a drop in yields and sown area led to a significant decline in the harvest for 1916. This compounded problems of supply that had been developing since 1914. Mass conscription of troops (mainly from peasant ranks) had left large areas of the land uncultivated, and food riots subsequently occurred in the capital.

Procurement agencies quickly sprang up after the onset of war in 1914 in order to provide supplies for military personnel. Nikolai Kondratiev wrote a major study of matters relevant to this topic entitled *The Grain Market and its Regulation During the War and Revolution* in 1918. Here he stressed the importance of recognising the structure of the pre-war Russian grain market to an understanding of wartime events, in particular the proportion of grain produced by peasants as against proprietors. Since the degree of marketability of grain differed between the two types of producer – peasants marketing far less of their crops – changes to production levels on proprietory farms would be crucial in determining the amount of grain available for wide distribution. In this heavy reliance on proprietory farms Kondratiev saw the roots of the catastrophic crisis that occurred in relation to food supply in Russia during the war. Other factors causing significant price rises were the fragmentation of transport links, declining credit facilities and a general fall in sown area.

Private trade in food supplies flourished on semi-legal markets during the war, causing some resentment amongst the urban population. A special Commissariat of Food was created in November 1917 as recognition of the importance of guaranteeing necessities in a conflict situation, and as a consequence of this situation the mentality of a shortage economy was burned into the minds of the Bolshevik government from the very beginning. However, Kondratiev emphasised that the new Bolshevik administration did not initially introduce any new policies regarding food supply, rather it preserved the basic elements of the policy of the Provisional Government, a grain monopoly having been previously introduced in March 1917. Hence with respect to the position vis-à-vis internal trade, the Bolsheviks inherited a rather grim food supply situation but had no particular policies, socialist or otherwise, prepared beforehand for dealing with it.

In October 1917, just before the Bolsheviks obtained control of state power, Lenin gave a clear indication of how he conceived of the socialist economy coming into being. He suggested that capitalism had created an appropriate accounting apparatus in the form of the banks, syndicates, the postal service, consumers' societies, and office employees' unions that could be taken over ready-made from capitalism and used to bring about socialism, by means of simply severing its capitalistically controlled head. Sometime before this, in May 1917, Lenin had directly linked the nationalisation of the banking system with social control of capitalist syndicates.[5] In this conception, countrywide accounting of production and distribution would be the skeleton of the new socialist society, and this would all be accomplished through a single legally sanctioned decree. In the event it would turn out that rather more than one decree was required to build a socialist economy.

## The war as analysed in socialist theory

Lenin's 'accounting apparatus' conception of socialism had its roots at least in part in his view of the underlying causes of war. According to Marxist theory, war was the result of imperialistic rivalry over colonial markets and was fought solely in the interests of international finance capital. Lenin's 1916 pamphlet *Imperialism as the Highest Phase of Capitalism* expressed this view at least indirectly, with the monopoly stage being conceived as in no way eliminating the competitive tendencies of capitalism. Lenin had been inspired in part by Hilferding's 1910 book *Finance Capital*, which had analysed the end of English economic supremacy in the world market. According to Hilferding the growth in the superior competition of Germany and America with respect to the export of capital led to a struggle for markets, which in turn became a conflict among national banking groups over spheres of investment for loan capital.[6] This led in turn to a more active colonial policy, to annexation of territory and to direct conflicts of interest between different states. That such economic conflicts might periodically erupt into war appeared to follow naturally. Alternative explanations of the origins of the war, such as the nature of the international diplomatic system or lingering grievances over previous wars, were downplayed.

During the war the power of the state over the economy grew significantly in many participating countries, alongside the growth of nationalistic sentiment, which was interpreted by some Marxists as proof that capitalist economy was ripe for transformation into socialism. Indeed Lenin explicitly highlighted the fact that imperialism was to be the final phase of capitalism, as resolving its contradictions within a framework of private ownership was seen as impossible. The rise in state control and the merging of previously distinct elements of capitalist economy had led Lenin to articulate his initial 'accounting apparatus' view of socialist economy. For example in his 1917 'April Theses', which set out the Bolshevik approach to the war, Lenin called for the immediate fusion of all the banks in the country into one general national bank, which could then exert full control over Russian financial affairs. This was presented as a deceptively simple and straightforward task, but in reality it would prove extremely complex and protracted to engineer.

As well as Lenin and Hilferding, the leading Bolshevik theorist Nikolai Bukharin had provided a significant wartime analysis of imperialism in his 1915 work *World Economy and Imperialism*. Here Bukharin provided a detailed account of the organisational forms of international capitalist economy and suggested that war was the immanent law of a society producing goods under the pressure of the spontaneously developing world market. The specific organisational forms that Bukharin had in mind were syndicates, cartels and trusts, behind which stood international finance capital. For example in Russia the number of highly developed syndicates and trusts exceeded one hundred, with the coal industry, the iron industry and oil being dominated by such organisations. According to one authority, nearly one half of all investment in industrial enterprises across the globe was in the form of cartels and trusts at this time.[7]

In general Bukharin believed that the war had acted to further centralise industrial production, with both horizontal concentration of small independent states and vertical centralisation among agrarian states occurring. Moreover he predicted that cooperation between state and private monopolies would be introduced after the war was over, and an overall strengthening of the economic activities of the state would occur. Bukharin called this tendency state capitalism, rather than state socialism or war socialism, since the existing class relations would not be altered.

However all these developments created a centralised production apparatus which, implicitly at least, could be taken over by the dictatorship of the proletariat and used for socialistic aims. Again like Lenin, Bukharin believed that capitalism itself was creating the centralised accounting mechanism that would be used in socialist planning, and hence no effort was required to think about this problem in detail before revolutionaries had achieved power. It is of course possible to conceive of an alternative scenario, in which socialist theorists did not believe that capitalism itself had created a socialist accounting system, and hence one had to be designed in detail before political control was achieved. This modification would be no guarantee of success in the new accounting task of course, but such an alternative approach might with hindsight appear more pre-scient.

## The general significance of 1917

A detailed examination of the political run of events that eventually pro-duced the Bolshevik *coup d'etat* are outside the scope of this book, but February and October 1917 undoubtedly marked decisive turning points in Russian political history. The old Tsarist order had crumbled to red dust amidst the fickle ravages of war, and after the Provisional Govern-ment had wavered fatally in the summer of 1917, a new cutting-edge revo-lutionary socialist government was installed. This Bolshevik government held in its hands the accumulated hopes of socialists not only in Russia but also of those across the entire globe. At last a real opportunity for creating fundamentally new 'egalitarian and efficient' non-capitalist forms of economy from scratch had arisen in a country richly endowed with raw materials and with the potential for positive development. The story of how this world-historical opportunity was partly smothered and also in large part squandered is one of the most important single threads running through the economic history of the twentieth century.

As already noted, it is a contention of this book that this opportunity was in part wasted not because of a lack of genuine and profound consideration of the issues by the thinkers charged with the task of design-ing the new socialist economic order. Rather an important component in the failure was the apparent blindness to large parts of the work of these thinkers exhibited by the people who controlled the levers of power. At the very least this element has subsequently been neglected by scholars, who have focused most emphatically on what actually happened rather than on what contemporaneous thinkers believed could (and perhaps should) have happened.

People who crave or revel in power are sometimes philosophically igno-rant, and hence are not always best suited to making decisions requiring deep theoretical understanding. In Soviet Russia the form of government adopted by the Bolsheviks, the rule of one political party, compounded this problem, as did the hostility of foreign governments such as the UK and the fact that the Bolsheviks themselves were ill-prepared for assuming economic control prior to 1917. In the remainder of this book the work of Soviet economists in debating the issues at hand, for example in selecting what planning methods to use and in designing various alternative economic formations, is analysed in its historical and institutional context. In what follows directly the first tentative steps taken by the Bolsheviks towards creating a socialist economy are examined.

## The first steps of the Bolshevik government

Revolutionary socialists had finally grasped state power in Russia, but what did they do with it in practical terms? As economic matters were central to socialist concerns, it might be thought that an economic transformation would receive first priority. Four key pieces of legislation especially relevant to the economy enacted soon after the Bolshevik assumption of power, i.e. in November/December 1917 and January 1918, were as follows:

1   decrees on workers' control;
2   the creation of a Supreme Council of the National Economy (VSNKh);
3   the nationalisation of the banks;
4   the socialisation of the land.

Russia's sizable foreign debt was also annulled, which (perhaps unsurprisingly) antagonised many foreign governments, especially those who held the debt. This policy could be seen to be as much a matter of expediency as of ideology, since funds were particularly scarce in wartime conditions. However, whilst the level of Russian foreign debt was approximately 16 billion rubles, the amount of internal debt was still higher, around 44 billion rubles.[8]

Taking each of the above elements in turn, the decrees on workers' control allowed workers to supervise industrial production through control councils, although proprietors still nominally retained ownership. Lenin had announced that genuine workers' control over production was an important goal of Bolshevik policy immediately after the October revolution, although the trades unions could in theory override this new form of control. However the anarchical tendencies of genuinely independent workers' councils proved difficult to manage and they soon attracted criticism from various sources. For example they were said to dissipate rather than concentrate control over production, this being interpreted negatively, and hence they soon faded in importance from Bolshevik plans for the economy. Moreover the phrase 'workers' control' was itself ambiguous, the Russian word *kontrol'* often connoting a meaning closer to supervision and oversight, rather than suggesting absolute authority over industrial affairs. Even in the more moderate sense, workers' supervision of industry did not feature for long in Bolshevik ideas.

The Supreme Council of the National Economy (VSNKh) was created in order to assist in the centralised control of various local institutions and to coordinate the activity of economic and political organs of management. Its goal was to organise all the activity of the national economy and state finances by elaborating general norms and the planned regulation of economic life, and it was initially composed of members of the Council of Workers' Control, representatives from the People's Commissariats and also consultant experts.[9] Its first president was Osinsky and its first bureau included Bukharin, Larin, Milyukov and Sokol'nikov. A later president of VSNKh, A.I. Rykov, declared revealingly in 1918:

> I have always thought that it was possible to organize a socialist *society* provided that there was an international socialist revolution; but to organize a socialist *branch of industry* ... excuse me, but hitherto no socialist has ever made such proposals, or can make them.[10]

Following on from this conception (which could easily be disputed), VSNKh implemented the centralisation of overall control without much attention to the question of what might constitute a socialist structure for individual enterprises. Creating an overarching mechanism for controlling the constituent elements of the Russian economy – enterprises, banks, trades unions and so on – was given priority over transforming the constituent elements themselves, at least in the first year of Soviet power. This priority was perhaps understandable, but had important consequences for many later developments.

The nationalisation of banks was designed to wrest control of the financial system away from private proprietors and into Bolshevik hands. The first decree on nationalisation issued on 27 December 1917 declared that all banking affairs were to become a state monopoly and that the function of the liquidation of enterprises would be transferred to the State Bank.[11] As outlined previously, Lenin initially believed that the large banks constituted the state apparatus that could be taken ready-made from capitalism and used for the realisation of socialism. In the event financial nationalisation proceeded *ad hoc* in fits and starts, through three layers of the Russian banking system; the State Bank, large joint-stock banks and various specialised banking institutions.[12] For example a second decree dated 24 January 1918 confiscated the share capital of private banks that had not been affected by previous nationalisation measures.[13] Again Lenin thought that a single State Bank with branches in every district and factory was initially the answer, but various acts of defiance and sabotage from within the banking system itself meant that troops had to be dispatched to occupy first the State Bank and then important private banks. The notion that nominal control of Russia's banking system was nine-tenths of what was needed for socialism was quickly revealed as naive.

The decree on the socialisation of the land, issued at the end of January 1918, declared that all land was henceforth transferred for the use of all working people. The right of private ownership of land, underground wealth, waterways, forests and the forces of nature was abolished forever. The general right to use land was to lie only with those who cultivated it with their own labour, and the employment of hired labour was made illegal. No individual person was to have more land than they could work themselves, or less than was needed for a decent life. In more specific terms a consumer-labour standard was to be employed in which the size of the new allocation was determined by a calculation involving the number of worker units and bread consumers involved, with a schedule equating men, women and children of various ages.[14] This decree decisively and effectively annulled the power of the land-owning class, their key asset having been confiscated.

However, the precise content of the decree on the socialisation of the land was the result not of prolonged theoretical cogitation on the best way forward in this respect, but was to an important extent the outcome of political horse-trading between the Bolsheviks and their closest rivals, the Socialist Revolutionaries. Moreover the process of the confiscation of landed estates had been developing spontaneously throughout the revolutionary period, and thus to some extent the Bolsheviks were trailing behind events. In addition the actual process of redistribution did not follow the principles laid out to any degree of accuracy, and the Bolsheviks themselves soon came to regard the decree as fatally flawed. Finally, it was found that the actual content of the decree was open to various different interpretations when implementation was actually attempted.

One general point to take from all this might be that, whilst the meaning of phrases such as 'workers' control' and 'land nationalisation' appeared reasonably clear and unambiguous when agitators proclaimed them at heated political meetings, when an attempt was made to actually implement such ideas in practice, it was discovered that such phrases were the tips of very deep and complex icebergs, which could easily gorge a gaping hole in the hull of the liner of socialist development.

## The nationalisation of industry

However it is perhaps a little surprising that the wholesale nationalisation of industry did not occur immediately after the Bolshevik assumption of power, given that socialised ownership was such an important plank of Marxist doctrine. In fact it did not begin to happen in full measure until June 1918, when SNK issued a decree nationalising all of the large and most important enterprises in industry and transport. Due to lack of means of control by VSNKh the decree initially rented back the enterprises to their former owners, although full control was eventually transferred to VSNKh in 1919. Also during 1919 nationalisation was extended to some medium and small enterprises.[15] According to VSNKh calculations, of the 6900 large enterprises employing 1,277,505 workers documented to be in existence, 4547 (or 65.9 per cent) had been nationalised by November

1920. Moreover the extent of nationalisation differed in different branches of industry. In the chemicals and paper sectors for example nationalisation was virtually complete by the end of 1920, but in the metalworking and mining sectors, 75 per cent of industry was still in private hands.[16]

Three stages in the actual progress of nationalisation have been identified. In the first stage, from November 1917 to February 1918, wildcat nationalisation was limited to certain regions such as the South West and central areas and to certain specific factories. In the second stage, from March 1918 to June 1918, the socialisation of some industrial branches began and the conditions for the nationalisation of all large-scale industry were created. In the third stage, following the SNK decree in June 1918 to the spring of 1919, the speed of nationalisation increased, many large-scale factories were targeted and attention was turned to some medium sized firms.[17] The policy of nationalisation was intended initially to be a gradual process, developing through various types of industry, but was speeded up by various contextual factors such as continuous pressure from below. Preparatory work, before nationalisation actually occurred, with the aim of preventing disruption in the manufacturing process, was sensibly envisaged by some, but was sometimes bypassed because of overeager participants.

Moreover, political conflicts between competing conceptions of how far and how fast nationalisation should go soon reared up, with some even proposing wholesale and immediate nationalisation of the entire national economy. A decree on overall nationalisation of all enterprises with as little as five workers was passed in November 1920, with the aim of resolving all the *ad hoc* and spontaneous developments that were occurring, but was only partially implemented. As summarised by Silvana Malle:

> If financial disorganisation, anti-market policies, civil war and the need for control over supply all accounted for the increased pace of nationalisation in 1919–20, the reasons for the decree on overall nationalisation of November 1920 have to be found, instead, in the conception of a central plan of supply of raw materials and consumer goods, which started taking shape in the course of the civil war, along with the rising rate of inflation and progressive demonetisations of the war economy.[18]

Additional factors to be added to this explanation include the fact that the concept of nationalisation was itself somewhat ambiguous, in that the precise form it might take was not specified in detail prior to 1917.

As nationalisation progressed the power and capacity of VSNKh as an institution to control industrial production increased, and it was correspondingly divided into various 'chief administrations' (*glavki*) or governing boards, which controlled enterprises of particular types or in particular branches. For example in a SNK decree dated 2 May 1918, control of all

nationalised sugar factories was declared to be through the central directorate sugar committee.[19] Moreover sections and committees were formed
within VSNKh as necessity demanded, and territorial divisions continued
to operate through a network of local councils. Regarding the individual
management of enterprises, in the early Soviet period an unlikely mix of
personnel was sometimes selected; a tailor to run a metallurgical concern
and a painter to run a textile factory for example.[20] Often such people
lacked the experience necessary, the accumulation of business knowledge
in local networks not being considered as important before 1917 in
Marxist doctrine. In relation to private trade itself, this was officially
banned on 21 November 1918.

In theoretical terms Lenin characterised the initial steps undertaken by
the Bolsheviks with respect to the economy as coming under the banner of
'state capitalism', or as an attempt to obtain state control of the leading
elements of capitalist economy, in order that the transition to socialism
could begin to be implemented. However this approach to economic
affairs was sidelined by the ensuing civil conflict, and state capitalism
quickly gave way to war communism.

## Alternatives to the first and intermediate steps

All the above developments occurred in piecemeal fashion over time,
partly in response to particular problems of management, partly to
strengthen the new government and partly as a result of the extension of
what was perceived as socialist-type control. But what was obviously
lacking from the start was a grand scheme of how to transform the
Russian economy into a socialist system; in fact no such scheme, grand or
otherwise, had ever existed. While Marxist theory had provided a quite
detailed account of the economic structures of capitalism, it had neglected
to provide a comprehensive account of the specific socialist formations
that would replace them. Hence the Bolsheviks were forced to improvise in
quite difficult circumstances as they went along. The economic structures
of the USSR were the result of this process, not of any preconceived over-
arching plan of action.

However, some individuals within the socialist movement had provided
various partial and incomplete accounts of how particular facets of socialist policy might unfold, and debates at the time of the revolution added
some new components. For example Kondratiev, as a leading member of
the Socialist Revolutionaries, had favoured the idea of 'all-people's property' with regards to land reform, rather than Bolshevik-type socialisation.
Centralised or state control of the land, which was ultimately implemented
by the Bolsheviks, was another option. Transferring land into the management of local peasant communes or cooperatives was certainly possible to
some extent, as might have been the designing of completely new agricultural institutions for collectively controlled land. Allowing a complex mix

of many different forms, even including the retaining of some private control of large-scale farms, was also an option.

That particular land reform policies could have favoured particular social strata against others in the short run might be true, but since genuine socialists should have been concerned with creating true equality for all, rather than supporting some groups against others, this might be thought a not insurmountable difficulty. Offering the Russian population a referendum with a range of land reform options to select from as the deciding mechanism might have been cumbersome, especially given the volatile situation, but in principle it might be thought that a direct democracy should take this type of approach to deciding the land issue.

Regarding the nationalisation of enterprises, the Bolsheviks quickly took this to mean the supreme right of the state to own and control the totality of the means of production as it saw fit. Thus nationalisation was conceived as the state-isation of industry through centralised control. Admittedly the state could use nationalised industry in various ways; it was suggested that the state could grant concessions to other organisations, or it could favour the socialisation or municipalisation of industry. Socialisation was defined as occurring when nationalised industry was employed by one or other social group or organisation, such as the private operation of social control through cooperatives.[21] By the autumn of 1918, 2612 industrial units had been nationalised against 576 that had been municipalised.

However, the centralised state control of industry was not the only option that was available for socialists to pursue. Alternatively, the control of industry could have been transferred into the hands of each individual factory to run itself spontaneously, as implied by one interpretation of the decrees on workers' control. Or control could have been vested in elected factory councils that coordinated activity with both planning agencies and consumer organisations in a horizontal network structure. Moreover, some elements of private control could have been retained, for example by keeping the existing stock of the company intact but redistributing the shares to workers, or to a general holding council or some other form of socialised control. That the centralising element was the most important to the Bolsheviks indicated that they placed naked power high on their list of priorities at this time.

One account of various forms of business enterprise published not long after 1917 discussed cooperative and socialist economic formations in detail. A general distinction was made between state economy, state socialism, cooperative socialism, collective forms of economy and planned economy. In cooperative socialism the control of all enterprises would be transferred to autonomous associations that would be controlled only by the employees themselves. In another conception socialism would entail not the creation of any new collective organisations, but rather would consist of simply the establishment of a new (more just and equitable) principle of the distribution of the fruits of economic activity. There was also specified different ways in which nominal control of the means of production in general could be held – by private, state, commune, or by a public self-governing unit.

It was further suggested in this brainstorming of alternatives that a mechanical conception of socialisation envisaged external organisations creating a new economic order through the formation of organs of self-regulation, whilst in a different view it was recommended that to overcome capitalism, the socialisation of the separate branches of the national economy individually would be required. State-isation, municipalisation, the creation of public-law organisations and even mixed enterprises combining elements of private and social control were also suggested as theoretical possibilities.[22] Thus there were many alternatives to Bolshevik economic policies outlined at the time, at least in theory if not always in practice.

## War communism, 1918–1920

In the event the October revolution was not the final stage of socialists taking control of Russia, as a bitterly fought civil war erupted soon after, with major consequences for the economy. The anti-Bolshevik forces within Russia received significant assistance from overseas, US support being contingent on the recognition of pre-war Russian debts.[23] Various factors conspired to engage the economic system that developed in parallel with the civil war and that became known as war communism. Shortages of food and other necessities, foreign control of large areas of the country, a British naval blockade, and the desire to defeat the anti-Bolshevik White Army all contributed to an important degree.

Perhaps the most significant element of war communism in economic terms was a compulsory requisitioning system for obtaining agricultural supplies, involving the confiscation of the rural household surplus over and above essential requirements. This was then distributed to urban consumers through a rationing schedule in order to provide for basic necessities. In general the various principles governing the war communist economy have been given as the maximum extension of state authority, the forced allocation of labour, the centralised management of economic activity, a class basis for distribution and the naturalisation of economic life.[24] In the spring of 1918, Lenin proposed the idea of applying Taylorism to Russian industry, suggesting that a drive for productivity was also seen as important at this time.

However, some economic thinkers went a step further and argued that in war communism, elements of a truly socialist order were being born. For example in June 1918 a decree nationalising all enterprises with capital of one million rubles or above was issued.[25] This was in part ideologically inspired, nationalisation being viewed as a key element of the socialist economic order, but previous debates about the nuances of what particular form socialised control of industry should take were in some measure disregarded by the Bolsheviks, who took a straightforward state-controlled view of social ownership. Moreover a devastating hyperinflation gripped the Russian economy after 1918, in part a continuation of Tsarist financial policies begun during the First World War, but once again some thinkers saw in this the beginnings of socialist economy and the end of monetary accounting in itself. E.A. Preobrazhensky famously characterised the paper currency printing press as a machine gun with which to shoot the bourgeoisie in the rear, demonstrating that politics had primacy over financial concerns in the minds of many Bolsheviks at this time.

A good example of the conception of military-style socialism that arose during the civil war was provided by Leon Trotsky's view of planned economy. In December 1919 Trotsky advocated labour armies for economic construction, which were designed strategically to place detachments of soldiers into the civilian economy. This process involved creating lists of army personnel with specific skills and then matching them to the relevant labour shortages. Moreover in January 1920 Trotsky proclaimed that the Third Army would be transformed wholesale into the First Revolutionary Labour Army, with centralised control, operational labour reports and competition between labour units. Trotsky also believed that strict military-style discipline should be used in the railway system, and that trade unions under socialism needed to be transformed into unions for production, given that social ownership had negated the need for workers' rights. Unpaid labour on 'communist Saturdays and Sundays' was encouraged, and ultimately trade unions were to be merged with the administrative apparatus of the developed socialist economy.[26] Whether this in reality amounted to a pernicious form of 'pseudo-socialist exploitation' is a matter for the reader to decide.

Trotsky had been a successful Commissar of War during the civil war and hence it is not surprising that his attitude to planning was strongly militaristic. However to what extent the experiences of the civil war period affected all early Bolshevik conceptions of socialist economy is a difficult question to answer in full. Given that Marxist theory even before 1917 was replete with metaphors of 'battle', 'struggle' and 'smashing' institutions like the state, it would be unfair to blame the Russian experience alone for the prevalence of the military-style model of planning, although some level of influence of this particular context must be acknowledged to have occurred.

The question of encouraging industrial development soon took the attention of Bolsheviks after the main plank of the civil war was over. In March 1920 a decision was taken (and supported by Lenin) to fund the import of railway equipment into Russia from overseas with significant gold expenditure. As a consequence 1200 new steam locomotives and 1500 tanker wagons eventually reached Russia between 1921 and 1924. In part this was a continuation of a Witte-type industrialisation programme, although during NEP a retreat from the grand objective of rapid economic reconstruction was forced upon the Bolsheviks.[27] In terms of strategy this railway import policy suggested that the modernisation of key branches of the economy was a central component of Bolshevik thinking at this time, this modernisation sometimes being confused with specific forms of socialist economy themselves.

## Financial and monetary planning

During war communism a campaign for the abolition of money as a means of accounting grew in strength, inspired in part by socialist doctrine but compounded by contextual factors such as the prolonged depreciation of the ruble and the disruption of monetary trading networks caused by war. A new unit of economic accounting was apparently required to replace paper money and its derivatives, and ideas such as a 'labour unit' or an 'energy unit' were initially greeted with enthusiasm. However nothing came of these ideas in practical terms, as events outstripped such considerations, although accounting by book entry only (rather than through paper currency) was common in certain settlement relations during the war communist period.

The NKFin economist L.N. Yurovsky discussed the theory of non-monetary forms of accounting in detail. Ideas such as employing a combination of labour-energy units – human labour, mechanical energy, diesel energy, raw materials and production equipment – were criticised for their inability to provide an unambiguous method of equating the different forms of outlay. Another idea, that of labour hours or the quantity of expended labour, involved measuring 'one hour of simply unqualified socially-necessary labour fulfilling 100 per cent of the norm', with a tariff schedule for different types of qualified labour. Yurovsky argued that the issue of deciding what was 'socially necessary' and what was 'the norm' meant that such schemes could prove no more than purely subjective methods of accounting, even without considering how to set the tariff relations, and hence were inferior to monetary forms of accounting through markets and prices. Chayanov's suggestion that the level of labour expenditure and the level of gross income should be set against the labour burden and the measure of consumer satisfaction was again conditional on the units chosen for measurement.[28]

However the idea that the monetary evaluation process that occurs via markets and through prices was somehow objective could be questioned. It could be argued that individual human valuation expressed through choices in the marketplace was itself a socially constructed and hence a subjective process, even when money was used as the universal equivalent.[29] From this point of view Yurovsky's criticisms of non-monetary accounting were correct, but his advocacy of monetary accounting was based on flawed reasoning. On the other hand, given that monetary accounting was well established as a habitual convention in the Russian economy, then it might be seen as reasonable to argue that it was easier to operate this form of valuation than non-monetary forms, but not that no subjectivity was involved in its measurement procedures.

## The first socialist economic formations

Various first attempts at creating socialist economic formations occurred both consciously and spontaneously at this time. For example *kombedy*, or committees of the poor peasantry, were set up in June 1918 to work out how to distribute grain between family units and the state, but these were abolished in December 1918. In industry, various groupings (*kusty*) were formed to connect local enterprises in a particular branch, which were then managed by the VSNKh central administration responsible for the area in question. The creation of industrial syndicates was sometimes encouraged, with management committees composed of both workers and factory owners, but was a limited phenomenon.

However, while there were many debates in areas such as how to control the state sector of the economy, how socialist financial policy might develop and how the peasantry might be included in Bolshevik command immediately following 1917, much less attention was paid to examining the internal composition of socialist forms of economy or of setting out how non-capitalist production relationships might develop. Taking a top-down approach, the Bolsheviks at least initially thought that overall control of existing structures would suffice, leaving the question of interior microstructure to resolve itself.

## The response from overseas

The response to the Bolshevik assumption of power from overseas governments was at least initially overwhelmingly hostile, as perhaps would be expected. However the question of trading with Bolshevik Russia soon arose, and in the UK steps were eventually taken to normalise trading relations, although in a context of declining export levels for Britain and the outbreak of crisis in both the UK and the USA.[30] An insight into the conception of the new Bolshevik system held amongst British government circles is available from a Board of Trade document guiding participants in negotiations over the resumption of trade with Russia from May 1920. The document opens with the statement that:

> The British Delegates should firmly refuse to be drawn into any discussions as to the respective merits of Individualism and Communism as the economic basis of society, as such discussions are bound to be sterile and will only prolong and probably envenom the negotiations.[31]

Whilst ruling groups in the UK were evidently prepared to re-engage practically with Russian trading organisations, they apparently feared the spread of communism as an economic basis of society that might occur even by discussing its possible merits or faults.

## Conclusion

By 1921 the civil war was over and the Bolsheviks had cemented their control of the Russian economy, which had suffered first an international war followed by two revolutions followed then by a bitterly fought domestic conflict. Also by 1921 various debates and discussions about aspects of socialist forms of economy had occurred, for example over forms of technical accounting and military planning, and important steps towards creating a particular type of socialist economy had been taken. How the Bolsheviks further developed these discussions into active policies throughout the 1920s, and how various economists continued to contribute to these debates, is the subject of the next chapter.

# 4   Bolshevik economy, 1921–1929

## Key developments in Russia and the West in the 1920s

The 1920s witnessed further significant developments in human intellectual and practical life across Europe and America. *Art deco* replaced *art nouveau* as the dominant style in the high arts, as symbolised by the opalescent glass of Rene Lalique, the chryselephantine sculptures of Demetre Chiparus and the striking macassar ebony and walnut used in the manufacture of much new furniture. In the world of *haute couture* Coco Chanel set the roaring twenties alight (at least in Paris) with her trend-setting 'little black dress'. In the scientific world Werner Heisenberg exploded what remained of mechanistic Newtonian physics in 1926 with his uncertainty principle, proving that both the precise position and momentum of a sub-atomic particle could not simultaneously be known; quantum mechanics proper was duly born. In philosophy Ludwig Wittgenstein published his *Tractatus Logico-Philosophicus* first in German in 1921 and in English a year later, in which the existent world was defined simply as everything that was the case.

In American economics John Commons investigated the *Legal Foundations of Capitalism* and their concrete manifestation in the working rules of going concerns, identifying the transaction as the ultimate unit of economic investigation. Wesley Mitchell founded the National Bureau of Economic Research in New York in 1920, this institute being devoted to studying business cycles empirically and to accurately identifying their peaks and troughs. Frank Knight made an important distinction between risk and uncertainty in relation to an understanding of the concept of profit and proposed consideration of five constituent elements of economic progress; population, capital, technology, business organisation and new wants. In the UK J.M. Keynes supported policies of both active monetary management and state investment in the economy, the latter being seen as a cure for unemployment, but was vigorously opposed by supporters of the Treasury view of sound money such as R.G. Hawtrey and A.C. Pigou.

Outside of the academic world Mickey Mouse was born courtesy of Walt Disney and Norma Jean Baker was born without much parental courtesy, wireless telegraphy was invented, insulin was first discovered and mies van der Rohe designed the Barcelona chair. While an atmosphere of decadent abandon had characterised most of the 1920s in Europe and America (at least for ruling elites and their acolytes), this would come to an abrupt and sobering end with the Wall Street Crash of 1929. Lalique did not subsequently produce lost wax vases decorated with stylised representations of stockbrokers leaping off tall office blocks.

In Russia in the 1920s a period of relative intellectual openness was observed, with socialist and non-socialist thinkers making many original contributions to areas such as linguistics, philosophy and of course economics. The arts in Russia also witnessed significant new developments such as constructivism in both architecture and design. While some Russian intellectuals had emigrated overseas after 1917, others decided to remain in Soviet Russia even though they might have had serious misgivings about the authoritarian nature of the regime. In the period immediately following 1917 it was by no means clear that the Bolshevik government would survive for any length of time, and hence some level of internal opposition was likely thought possible by many.

## The new economic policy, 1921–1929

The civil war came to an end in 1920 with a Bolshevik victory, and various economic consequences duly followed. It was Lenin himself who was the mastermind behind the New Economic Policy and the concomitant introduction of market elements into Bolshevik economy. Indeed as the most important advocate of NEP, without the support of Lenin it is unlikely that such a thoroughgoing *volte face* would have been so successfully embraced by the Bolsheviks. The first element of NEP was the replacement of the grain requisitioning of war communism by a tax in kind, adopted in a government decree of 21 March 1921. Others elements which subsequently appeared were concessions to foreign companies, attempts to reintroduce a stable currency, decrees to privatise some industrial enterprises and the encouragement of party cadres to learn to trade successfully. NEP eventually brought about a general economic recovery, although this recovery was somewhat uneven and certainly hard-won.

Each component of NEP had its theoretical justification in party and non-party doctrine, and various economists were involved in this process to varying degrees. For example Bukharin provided ideological justification for the reintroduction of market elements generally into the Soviet economy, Preobrazhensky analysed the link between price policy and socialist accumulation, and Yurovsky played a key role in designing and implementing the monetary reform of 1922–1924 which introduced a new gold-backed currency, the *chervonets*. The work of these particular economic thinkers is further discussed in later sections of this chapter.

During NEP some crucial events influenced the economic policies being pursued by the Soviet government. One of these crucial events was the scissors crisis of 1923, which involved sharp movements in the relative prices of agricultural and industrial goods. As outlined by R.W. Davies, for four years following the scissors crisis one of the main planks of Soviet economic policy was to manipulate the relation between agricultural and industrial prices so as to direct resources into the development of state industry.[1] However this policy involved using fiscal, credit and price policies in combination, i.e. instruments of a market-based monetary system. This was control through the market rather than through direct planning, a fact of NEP life that increasingly irritated many Communist Party personnel, even though this was the defining feature of NEP itself.

Lenin's view on the importance of NEP was clear and based primarily on economic reasoning. In April 1921 he wrote:

> Socialism is inconceivable without large-scale capitalist engineering based on the latest discoveries of modern science ... At present petty-bourgeois capitalism prevails in Russia, and it is one and the same road that leads from it to both large-scale state capitalism and to socialism ... Those who fail to see this are committing an unpardonable mistake in economics.[2]

Thus state capitalist economy was not necessarily seen as an enemy of the USSR at this time, and Lenin fatefully associated socialism directly with large-scale production. As was noted in Chapter 2, in 1899 Lenin had disassociated the market as a category of political economy from capitalism as a system of control, thus assisting doctrinally with the reintroduction of market elements into Bolshevik economy during NEP.

## What exactly was a socialist society?

What exactly was the nirvana of socialist society that the Bolsheviks were trying to achieve after 1917? If they were committed to creating a planned economy then this must fit in with a more general conception of what socialism as a new type of civilisation really meant. As noted previously, there was no clear, generally agreed and all-inclusive document that could act as a blueprint for the construction of a socialist society in existence prior to 1917. Marx had rather elusively implied that such 'castles in the air' were not really necessary or even possible, although he had given various pointers on this matter such as that all property must be owned collectively and that planning must satisfy the needs of all, rather than only the needs of a few social groups. Engels had rather understatedly referred to planning as 'child's play', implying that all would become clear once socialists had obtained power. A harsh-sounding but transitional 'dictatorship of the proletariat' was to govern in the initial period of socialism, but this would then give way (after the complete abolition of all classes) to the full inclusion of all members of society in the political process. Exactly how this would occur was not however specified in detail.

In the event the question of how planning should function proved an extremely complex and protracted issue to resolve successfully, and the collapse of the Soviet system in 1991 might suggest that it never was adequately tackled. And this question was part of a broader issue of the nature of socialist society generally, which was also a very difficult problem to resolve. Marx had suggested that the socialist state could act as a neutral body in the interests of all members of society, but the Soviet governmental bureaucracy was quickly found to have its own motivations and interests that were not necessarily those of all the other members of society in unison. The rather utopian notion of Marx's that in socialism a person could work as a hunter, a fisherman, a shepherd and a critic all at the same time was not often mentioned by leading Bolsheviks after 1917, the harsh realities of life in a predominantly peasant country making a cruel mockery of Marx's utopian vision of future communist society.

A crucial element of socialist society, it might be thought by many, must surely be individual human social relations. The restructuring of capitalist social relations and the requirement not to use any existing social relations for exploitative or unjust aims might be perceived to be a crucial element of socialist society, just as important as the restructuring of property relations was seen to be. In fact leading Bolsheviks paid little attention to this issue after 1917, perhaps because they benefited from the new (but still unequal) social relations that came into existence after this date. Cynical readers might want to label such Bolsheviks as 'socialists of the self-interest', i.e. as being concerned with socialist ideology only to the extent that wealth and power is transferred from others to them, but being not nearly so concerned with such equalisation when any existing advantage might need to be taken away from them and given to others in order to achieve fair play. Even so, some economic thinkers in the NEP period were concerned with genuinely fostering new economic ideas, and attention will be focused on them in detail later in this chapter. But before this an account of some of the empirical features of Bolshevik economy is required, together with a consideration of some possible alternative approaches to economic development that were outlined by economists during NEP.

## The management institutions of NEP

The most important institutions of NEP charged with managing various aspects of the economy were as follows. VSNKh was the Supreme Council of the National Economy, STO was the Council of Labour and Defence and SNK was the Council of People's Commissars. Gosplan was the State Planning Commission, the designated organ for designing economic plans, and Gosbank was the State Bank. Key government ministries included the

People's Commissariats of Finance (NKFin), Agriculture (NKZem), Heavy Industry (NKTyazhProm), and Internal and Foreign Trade (NKVnu-VneshTorg). Within particular commissariats sub-departments such as the Conjuncture Institute, part of NKZem, were also significant, as were the republican branches of the various commissariats.

Each particular management organ fought for maintaining and extending its own power base throughout NEP, and economists attached to each organ likewise had strong institutional loyalty. For example Gosplan grew in importance during NEP as enthusiasm for the planning effort gathered momentum, and consequently Gosplan economists also grew in stature as NEP progressed. Such status dynamics were a double-edged sword however, as once a particular person had reached their apogee, there was often only one possible direction to follow onward from this.

From a structural point of view the management institutions of NEP reflected the mixed economy of NEP itself. The Communist Party asserted its political control through party conferences and congresses, the general resolutions and directives of which fed through directly to the more specialised organs such as Gosplan and VSNKh. However such directives were produced within a framework of relative economic freedom, and were usually only concerned with the general principles of control, and hence were often more indicative than imperative in nature. For Carr the introduction of NEP had required not so much the creation of new institutions as the transformation of the existing institutions of compulsion into instruments of encouragement.[3] In part this was true, but it also failed to highlight the fact that in NEP the institutions were continually evolving, both in structure and function, and that new economic ideas were certainly frequently forthcoming.

## Economic formations in NEP

Even though NEP was based on the reintroduction of market elements into Soviet society, it might be thought that some attempts at creating new economic formations might have occurred in the 1920s. One very significant development that occurred was that a system of industrial trusts and syndicates was recreated in many branches of the Soviet economy, although as state organisations under government control, indirectly at least. By the end of 1922 there were 426 trusts (such as the flax trust) composed of factories occupied in the same type of production, and also 20 syndicates. The organisation and status of trusts was defined in a decree of 23 May 1923, where they were recognised as distinct judicial entities with an autonomous nature founded on a commercial basis. A syndicate was a combination of trusts operating in a particular branch of the economy, for example in the oil and textile sectors.[4] Other new developments that occurred were the creation of industrial congresses, which were conventions of representatives of all trusts, and the formation of mixed enterprises, in which the state participated by means of its holdings of land, buildings and so on, but which in other ways operated like private companies.

With respect to the land, in May 1922 a government decree was issued which recognised the *artel*, the commune, the *mir* and various other types of smallholdings as equally valid forms of peasant organisation. With regard to industry, decrees were issued pronouncing an intention of encouraging small-scale industry and of cutting bureaucracy, and also of enabling the leasing of enterprises into private hands. By September 1922, 3800 small enterprises in areas such as the food industry had been leased, with rent paid as a percentage of goods produced. VSNKh still retained under its direct administration a number of large or strategically important industrial enterprises, but others were leased to private holdings in various forms. What was called 'economic accounting' (*khozraschet*) was to be the principle of operation of all industrial units in NEP, which meant that strict commercial principles of profit and loss were to be employed. Exactly how such commercial accounting was irrational in capitalist economy, but perfectly correct in Bolshevik economy, was not fully explained, except to say that revolutionaries were now in command and were directing the construction of socialism. Perhaps ends and means were being distinguished in an absolute manner.

With regards to business/consumer relations, trade in NEP was structured into three component areas; private, cooperative and state trading organisations. A corresponding division of realms grew up in which private trade dominated the retail sector, state trade dominated in the wholesale sector and cooperative trading organisations operated in both areas to varying extents.[5] In terms of institutions, various different trading conventions were common in the different sectors outlined. It might be thought that in the private sector, individual gain was the driving force, whereas in the state sector, concern for human welfare was the overriding aim. In cooperatives perhaps a mixture of motivations could be found, although in reality a complex set of guiding forces acted in all the different types of trade that existed. Regarding the relative success of the different forms of trade, private traders often had the edge with respect of the speed of turnover of goods, in part because private activity was often closest to the experience of the consumer on a daily basis.

## Financial policy during NEP

After the transition to NEP in 1921 the focus of Bolshevik financial policy shifted to stabilising the ruble and re-affirming monetary forms of accounting. At the end of 1921 a currency reform occurred that replaced 10,000 old rubles with one new one, and in the middle of 1922 a new gold-backed currency, the *chervonets*, was issued which circulated alongside the ruble. One *chervonets* equalled ten gold rubles and was (at least nominally) covered 25 per cent by precious metals and 75 per cent by other financial assets. The complete turnaround in financial policy that the introduction of the *chervonets* signified compared to previous discussions about the abolition of money cannot be overemphasised. Bolsheviks became unlikely but enthusiastic converts to 'sound money' and balanced budgets, something that can be explained in part by their victory in the civil war and the concomitant realisation that their government could last for a significant period of time. It was Lenin himself who was the guiding force behind the transition to NEP and he had proved himself ready and willing to warn of the dangers of bureaucratisation of the economy that botched planning efforts might enliven.

As a consequence, one of the most important topics for Soviet economists in the early years of NEP was that of currency reform. The hyperinflation of the ruble and the introduction of the new parallel currency, the *chervonets*, had led to much theoretical work on the relation between the issue of currency and inflation. NKFin economists such as L.N. Yurovsky were the guiding force behind the creation of the *chervonets*, but many others worked on the theory of inflation and on understanding the dynamics of a dual currency system. For example S.A. Falkner published a historical study entitled *Paper Money in the French Revolution, 1789–97* in 1919, and a book on Soviet emission called *Problems of the Theory and Practice of Emission Economy* in 1924. Preobrazhensky's *Theory of a Depreciating Currency* was not published until 1930, while Yurovsky's *Monetary Policy of Soviet Power* appeared in 1928.

Kondratiev had written a short account of the Soviet hyperinflation in terms of a simplistic version of the quantity theory of money in 1922, while Slutsky undertook a much more sophisticated analysis in terms of rigorously defined models and detailed scrutiny of the available data. The impetus for Slutsky's work in this area may have come from a concern that existing studies of the Soviet currency question were overly simplistic and lacked technical rigour. Thus policy decisions were being made by government organs such as NKFin without a proper understanding of what was actually happening to the ruble. Slutsky might have hoped that his analysis would provide policy-makers with a much clearer understanding of the current situation.

A short account of Falkner's article 'Past and Future Russian Emission Systems' of 1923 is revealing in this respect. Falkner attempted to evaluate Soviet emission policy by calculating what he called the absolute and relative effectiveness of emission. Absolute effectiveness was the real value of paper money emitted per month, calculated in terms of an index at the end of the month. Relative effectiveness was the percentage of the real value of commodity-money turnover elicited through emission per month. Falkner provided a graphical representation of these measures for Russia between 1918 and 1923, which he used to formulate the hypothesis that the portion of circulating commodity values elicited with the help of emission was proportional to the rate of emission. The more stable was the actual rate of emission, the more smooth and uniform was the growth of the money mass, and hence the higher was the relative effectiveness of emission. On the other hand, the more sharply the rate of emission changed, the lower was the effectiveness of the emission apparatus.[6]

Falkner outlined four basic stages in the history of Russian currency emission from 1916 to 1922 as follows. From the beginning of 1916 to mid-1919, the average rate of emission was around 6 to 7 per cent per month; from mid-1919 to mid-1921 the rate was around 15 per cent per month; from mid-1921 to mid-1922 the rate was highly volatile, the overall average for this period being 51 per cent per month; from September 1922 onwards a more stable rate of 32 per cent per month was seen. A close correspondence between the rate of emission and relative effectiveness, as shown by the data, was taken by Falkner as a confirmation of his hypothesis. He concluded by stressing that the stability of the rate of emission, and hence the gradualness of the decline in the value of monetary units, was a basic postulate of practical policy in relation to the expedient use of the emission apparatus for policy-related ends.[7] This work on Soviet currency emission was similar to work done by some Western economists such as those in Germany, where hyperinflation had also caused much damage during the First World War.

## Some alternatives to Bolshevik ideas

Given that NEP was a period of relative intellectual openness, it might be assumed that discussion of economic alternatives flourished, and some such variant ideas were indeed proposed. For example in relation to Soviet industrialisation strategy, Kondratiev and some other important Conjuncture Institute members (Vainshtein and Shaposhnikov) advocated the idea of increasing Soviet grain exports to provide the funds for future industrial development. Such funds would then be used to import advanced equipment from overseas in order to upgrade the Soviet capital stock, equipment that would cost much more to manufacture domestically.[8] A tax policy designed to encourage the peasantry to increase production levels and marketability went alongside this view, as did the idea (supported by People's Commissar Krasin) of encouraging foreign capital to invest in some parts of Soviet industry.

This package of policies could be called a market-led industrialisation strategy, and it fitted in with the theory of comparative advantage as employed in the classical theory of international trade. Later in the twentieth century it would be referred to as a policy of private sector led export-oriented growth, in contrast to the state-led import-substitution approach adopted by Stalin, although policies of what were called 'market-friendly' interventions to overcome specific market failures were also employed in export-led strategies. Some outside of the Conjuncture Institute, such as

L.N. Litoshenko, even supported the idea of transferring the ownership of land to those peasants who were strongest, i.e. they tacitly supported the restoration of private ownership.

Other alternative approaches were also developed. Within Gosplan Groman formulated a programme of economic progress based on the idea of a dynamic equilibrium between the development of the productive forces, generating individual human well-being, the creation of socialist forms of economy and maintaining a continually evolving balance. For example Groman specified a ratio of 37:63 for the percentage distribution of total sales between agricultural and industrial products for 1924–1925, this ratio being subsequently criticised for elevating a temporary empirical relation to a law-governed regularity. Groman received some theoretical support from Bazarov, although the idea of maintaining a genetic balance in the economy was eventually discarded by Gosplan in favour of a more teleological will-based conception of planning.

Within the People's Commissariat of Agriculture Chayanov analysed the structure and function of the family-labour farm in detail. In Chayanov's account of household agriculture, the balance between work accomplished and needs satisfied was the defining feature of such forms of economy. From this analysis Chayanov subsequently provided a general operative principle for a communist economy, which was that the exertion of social labour power should be taken to the point where the equilibrium between drudgery of labour and social demand satisfaction had been reached. This nodal point would be established by state planning organs, although a specific methodology for this was not provided by Chayanov.[9] It will subsequently be apparent from the next chapter that Soviet planners in the 1930s did not consider the drudgery of labour factor in the planning equation at all.

Moreover by 1927, Chayanov had outlined an original notion of cooperative collectivisation as the future for Soviet agriculture, which involved the gradual separation of sectors of specialisation away from individual households, and their organisation as public enterprises. This would enable both the horizontal concentration of peasant holdings into large-scale agricultural collectives, and also assist their vertical concentration into state economy through a centralised cooperative system of control.[10] In some ways Chayanov's idea of cooperative collectivisation linked in with Lenin's 1923 article 'On Cooperation', where agricultural cooperatives were identified as crucial to further progress towards socialism, although since Lenin had died in 1924, he was not able to provide any active support for Chayanov's alternative approach.

In other cases while explicit alternatives might not have been developed, it is possible to hypothesise that alternatives could have been developed with the theoretical tools that were then available. For example A.A. Bogdanov's ground breaking work on tektology – roughly meaning the general structures of control – first developed just before 1917 was of much relevance to designing systems of economic management. Tektology was the science of complex wholes, being concerned primarily with structural regularities and systemic types, and also with the laws of organisation of concrete forms of control. For Bogdanov the content of human life summed to the organisation of the forces of nature, the organisation of human forces and also of experience, the first two being particularly relevant to economic planning.[11] Such a prototype systems theory could have been gainfully employed in the design of new Soviet economic formations if those in charge had not been wilfully blind to Bogdanov's contribution, such blindness being in the main politically conditioned.

For example, the idea that organisations were structured through purpose and were devoted to overcoming particular resistances through directed activities had been applied by Bogdanov to elementary cooperation. The specific mode of combination of labour was identified as crucial as to whether favourable outcomes occurred; the more harmonious the combination, the more positive the outcome, and the higher the level of organisation.[12] It goes without saying that the Bolsheviks were not interested in even trying to apply such ideas to designing the cooperative institutions that they claimed were required, the organisational harmony of members rarely being seen as a factor to be considered at all by Soviet planners in the 1930s.

## Key economic thinkers of the period

Perhaps the richest vein that can be mined from NEP related to attempts to create new economic theory in relation to the new forms of economy that were coming into being. As already suggested, a significant number of groups and individuals made major contributions to new economic thinking in Russia between 1921 and 1929. These included policy-related groupings such as Bukharin and the Bukharinites and Kondratiev and associated economists in the Conjuncture Institute; institutional groupings like Strumilin, Groman and Bazarov in Gosplan and Sokol'nikov and Yurovsky in NKFin; and politically-based alliances such as Preobrazhensky and the Left Opposition. Various important individuals such as Slutsky, Chayanov, Bogdanov and Kantorovich must also be considered. The work of many of these economists was at least in part sponsored by the state, i.e. many were members of government departments such as NKFin and NKZem, although a few worked in relative isolation in mainly academic-related posts.

The economists covered in the rest of this chapter were best known for the following contributions. Bukharin was famous for theorising the war communist economy and for his subsequent enthusiastic support of the introduction of market elements into Soviet society. Some key Bukharinite associates included A. Aikhenvald, A.I. Stetsky and A. Slepkov. As already outlined Kondratiev developed a market-led industrialisation strategy for the USSR, in opposition to the state-led approach eventually chosen by Stalin, and also pioneered the development of business cycle analysis in Russia. Within the Conjuncture Institute Kondratiev was very ably deputised by A.L. Vainshtein and N.N. Shaposhnikov and further assisted by A.A. Konyus, I.N. Leontiev and N.S. Chetverikov. Strumilin, Groman and Bazarov worked on planning techniques and methodology and on understanding empirical developments in the Soviet economy from within Gosplan.

Sokol'nikov and Yurovsky analysed the role of money, banking and finance in a socialist economy and the principles of planning in general. Preobrazhensky developed the idea of 'pumping over' resources from the peasant to the state sectors of the economy and the concomitant notion of 'primitive socialist accumulation'. Slutsky analysed the effects of the emission of paper money and the application of mathematical statistics to economic theory. Chayanov worked on understanding the structure of peasant farms and the behaviour of those working in them. And Kantorovich analysed the role of supply and demand in a socialist economy and subsequently developed the idea of optimal planning. In what follows elements of this impressive range of work will be analysed in more detail, starting with Bukharin.

## N.I. Bukharin and the general justification of NEP

Nikolai Ivanovich Bukharin (1888–1938) joined the Bolshevik party in 1906. After being arrested in Moscow in 1911 he escaped abroad and settled in Vienna, where he studied the Austrian school of economics and subsequently wrote a critique of their work. Bukharin returned to Moscow in May 1917 and was elected to the party's Central Committee three months before the October revolution. He edited the authoritative newspaper *Pravda* from December 1917 to April 1929. In 1918 Bukharin positioned himself on the left of the party over Brest-Litovsk, but after 1921 he changed his attitude noticeably and became a leading figure on the right. In 1937 he was expelled from the party for political crimes and a year later he was sentenced to death.

Bukharin is perhaps most famous as a theorist for his general advocacy of the market during NEP. However, he never explicitly stated that the market was compatible with socialism, or that it would be used after the transition period was completed. He stuck to the doctrine that socialism ultimately required a planned economy. His only criticism of those enthusiastic for planning was that it was too soon to be discussing it during the early 1920s. However, as to the type of planning Bukharin favoured, it is possible to argue that it was a less rigid form than that which was finally adopted. It is also possible to argue that Bukharin's acceptance of the function the market performs in an economy should have led him, if he was being intellectually consistent, to reject imperative planning entirely in favour of some use of the market in socialism. The powerful grip that Bolshevist doctrine had upon his intellect was one factor that must have made such a step extremely difficult. In the sections that follow these points are outlined in more detail.

For Bukharin in the mid-1920s the key question was the *smychka* (connecting link) between workers and peasants.[13] In order to maintain Soviet power the *smychka* had to be preserved at all costs, as peasants were often hostile to Bolshevik control. Thus the crucial question was how to industrialise and how to build socialism while maintaining the *smychka*, NEP being a response to this problem. However, it is important to realise that for Bukharin the policies of NEP had both a political and an economic rationale. If the need to preserve the *smychka* was the political aspect of the argument, then the need to accumulate resources for industrialisation provided the economic rationale.

Bukharin expounded the basic economic argument for the policies of NEP in his 'Critique of the Economic Platform of the Opposition' of 1926. The Left Opposition saw the problem as a zero-sum game. The task was to transfer as much of a given amount of resources as was feasible into the hands of the state, and this was to be done by increasing prices of industrial products. However, according to Bukharin they neglected the central problem of economic life, which was speed of turnover of goods. The way to maximise state funds was in fact to lower industrial prices, which would increase the speed of turnover and thus increase the profit taken by the state.[14] A smaller percentage profit taken from a growing national product would be superior to a larger profit taken from a static or even declining national product. Thus according to Bukharin lowering industrial prices would both increase the accumulation fund and help to preserve the *smychka* between workers and peasants.

For Bukharin the question then arose of how the elimination of capitalist elements from the Soviet economy would eventually occur. This would happen by way of economic displacement:

> Private capital is not ... chopped off with a single sweep of the revolutionary sword ... It is overcome in the process of an economic struggle on the basis of growth in our state institutions and cooperatives; they squeeze out private capital economically.[15]

Thus Bukharin proposed an economic battle in which those who produced the best quality goods at the lowest prices would be the victors. For example in 'Concerning the New Economic Policy and Our Tasks' of 1925 he asked: how were private capitalists to be squeezed out? He answered 'By means of competition, and economic struggle. If they sell cheaply, we must reach a position where we can sell still more cheaply'.[16] Thus the question of individual incentive was seen by Bukharin to be central, and competition between state and private sectors was (at least in theory) to be a driving force of the transitional NEP economy.

## Bukharin and the market in the transition period

In this section how Bukharin thought the market would be utilised in the transition period will be examined. In 'The Path to Socialism and the Worker-Peasant Alliance' of 1925 Bukharin gave a good general statement on this question. He wrote:

> We thought that we would be able to destroy market relations immediately ... It has turned out that we are approaching socialism precisely through market relations. One could say that market relationships will be destroyed as a result of their own development.[17]

Bukharin reasoned on the self-negating property of the market as follows. In capitalism it was a general rule that large-scale production drove out small, with the market itself causing the number of competitors to decline. This was happening, and would continue to happen, in the USSR. Since the working class in alliance with the peasantry had taken control of large-scale production, private trade was left with only small-scale production, and thus would be ousted by large-scale state industry. As this process unfolded 'the market itself will sooner or later wither away, being replaced by the state-cooperative distribution of everything that is produced'.[18] The advantages of large-scale production would become more and more apparent with steadily growing economies of scale, and benefits would also accrue to state economy from the growth of planning.

Parallel with the idea of using the market to reach socialism, Bukharin developed his notion of 'growing into' socialism. Such an organic metaphor obviously implied that the process would occur over some period of time and would result in strong links between the constituent elements. The key question this theory answered was how to bring the peasant economy into socialism. In 'Concerning the New Economic Policy and Our Tasks' of 1925 Bukharin wrote:

> if the peasant was drawn into the system of industrial and banking capital through cooperative organisations, then, given our dictatorship and ... the nationalisation of the land, the peasant will be able to grow gradually into our system of socialist relations through cooperation.[19]

Using individual economic interest, cooperation was to attract the peasantry by giving them immediate advantages, for example by offering cheap credit through the state banking system. Or, in the case of a prosperous peasant who wanted to accumulate funds, by giving them higher interest rates in the state savings bank. Thus the peasant became interested in the stability of the state bank and consequently the Soviet regime, and through such links the 'growing in' process would develop. Although the 'growing in' metaphor was used primarily to describe the development of peasant economy, Bukharin used it in other areas too, for example the law of value 'growing into' the law of labour outlays. In fact this process was characteristic of the transition period as a whole, and it is clear that this slow, organic conception of the transition differed to quite a large extent from the conception of 'struggle' favoured by the Left.

Bukharin freely admitted that his conception of the transition involved using market methods of economic management. However, this did not mean that the Soviet economy could be described as capitalist; although the form was capitalistic, the content transcended the market. This seemed to imply that capitalist and market forms could be used in a socialist manner. Although Bukharin explicitly denied that the market could be used in socialism, the logic of his argument for its use in the transition implicitly made the case for precisely this combination. Given proletarian state control of the market, it could be regulated in a socialist manner, something that his more orthodox critics were quick to pick up on. In this respect one of Bukharin's most significant theoretical opponents was Preobrazhensky, to which attention is now turned.

## E.A. Preobrazhensky and primitive socialist accumulation

Evgeny Aleksandrovich Preobrazhensky (1886–1937) joined the RSDLP when he was 17 and in 1920 was elected to the Central Committee of the Communist Party. A leading member of Leftist oppositional factions in the 1920s he was most famous as a Marxist theorist of the NEP economy and for his controversial notion of 'primitive socialist accumulation'.

In his most important work, *The New Economics* of 1926, Preobrazhensky outlined a framework for understanding price policy in the transition to socialism. In the chapter on the law of value in Soviet economy he wrote:

> While on the capitalist market under free competition price is a function of value, the state-monopolist's price on the private market is a function of primitive socialist accumulation, limited by the law of value.[20]

According to Preobrazhensky there were two regulating laws in the Soviet economy of the transition period – the law of value and the law of primitive socialist accumulation – and these two laws were engaged in a struggle for dominance. Thus price, as both a regulator of production and a means for state accumulation, was one of the arenas of struggle between the two laws. Preobrazhensky's notion of primitive socialist accumulation, which caused much debate in Bolshevik ranks, was a means by which the state could accumulate funds for socialist construction by 'pumping over' resources from one sector to another. Prices of state-industry produced goods should be regulated in order to achieve this goal. However, as the quote above indicated, Preobrazhensky believed that this operation was limited by the law of value, which still at least partially functioned in the Soviet economy at this time.

Preobrazhensky gave an example of such price manipulation as follows. In areas where the state was a monopsonist (i.e. several sellers but only one buyer) such as industrial crops and raw materials, it could use its monopsonist position to regulate the prices it paid for these commodities. However, there existed two barriers established by the law of value. The maximum barrier was the average world price, the minimum barrier was the expenditure on labour and profitability for the producer as compared with other crops, resulting in a field of manoeuvre of 30–40 per cent below the world price. The difference between the procurement price which would be formed on the basis of free competition and the level actually paid by the Soviet state 'should be fully attributed to the operation of the law of primitive socialist accumulation'.[21] In the transition period, according to Preobrazhensky, not only would prices be used in order to facilitate socialist accumulation, but also to determine production priority in the peasant sector. He wrote:

> the price policy of the state, as the predominant purchaser, can have a profound influence on the distribution of the production forces in the peasant economy, encouraging certain crops at the expense of others and introducing an element of planning into the territorial distribution of crops in peasant economy.[22]

Here price was transformed from a category of commodity economy into something transitional towards socialist calculation.

Some have argued that, while Preobrazhensky himself was a victim of the purges at the end of the 1920s, his general idea of 'pumping over' was then surreptitiously employed by Stalin to extract resources from the peasant sector throughout the 1930s. There might be a limited metaphorical sense in which this was true, but Preobrazhensky did not advocate using coercive means to achieve such goals, and others have argued that collectivisation did not really enable the extraction of resources at all.

## L.N. Yurovsky and the theory of planning

L.N. Yurovsky (1884–1938) studied first at St Petersburg, Munich and Berlin, subsequently submitting a dissertation to Kharkov University on grain exports in 1913. In 1922 he became deputy president of currency management in NKFin and head of the currency section a year later. He was arrested at the beginning of the 1930s and accused of plotting capitalist restoration, finally being executed in 1938. While on the face of it Yurovsky was an orthodox neoclassical theorist, elements of institutionalism could also be detected in his work, as will be seen further on.

For example Yurovsky wrote a long article in 1926 entitled 'On the Problem of the Plan and Equilibrium in the Soviet Economic System', in which he examined the question of economic equilibrium in relation to the type of planning methodology being adopted in organs such as Gosplan. He began by stating that:

> The methodology of planned economy and the significance of the plan must clearly depend on the particularity of the economic system for which it is composed. An economic plan composed in 1926/7 is something principally different to the type of plan which we had in mind to compose in 1920.[23]

It is thus clear that Yurovsky believed that planning *per se* was not a type of economic system, and that the question of what constituted planning was at least somewhat divorced from the question of what constituted an economic system. This meant that it would theoretically be possible to have some form of planning in all types of economic system, and that the presence or absence of planning in an economic system was not necessarily its defining feature.

Yurovsky continued his analysis by outlining that since in Soviet conditions large parts of the means of production were held by the state, it was necessary to compose programmes of work for these state enterprises. Hence economic plans, such as a production plan, a transport plan and so on, were composed. Since the state also had a foreign trade monopoly, export and import plans were required in order to satisfy the demand for foreign goods. Thus the state budget had to be composed with all these factors in mind, and Yurovsky explained that this 'flows from the fact that the state owns the greater part of the country's productive forces'.[24] From this it is apparent that Yurovsky was arguing that property relations were a key defining feature of an economic system, and determined whether and to what extent and type planning occurred. This was confirmed by a statement that the necessity of planning flowed from the unprecedented concentration of means of production and other material resources into the hands of the state.

Yurovsky then discussed the notion of equilibrium. He explained that while in a capitalist economy equilibrium was broken and restored spontaneously, in the Soviet system equilibrium could be disturbed by a mistaken composition or implementation of a plan, and thus must subsequently be restored by conscious measures.[25] Yurovsky outlined various disproportions that he saw in the Soviet economy. First, there was a disproportion between the speed of restoration of agricultural and industrial production on the one hand, and the speed of restoration of foreign trade on the

other. According to Yurovsky foreign trade lagged behind domestic production by several decades, reaching only the levels of the 1880s.[26]
Another disproportion was that between wholesale and retail prices, and
also between state/cooperative prices and prices on private markets. In the
latter case Yurovsky noted the existence of a dual price structure, which
signified that, at the lower price level, it would be impossible to satisfy all
demand, and this meant that prices were not fulfilling their function as
equilibriators of supply and demand.[27]

Yurovsky analysed Preobrazhensky's book *The New Economics* in
detail. In his concrete description of the new Soviet economy, Yurovsky
believed that Preobrazhensky was absolutely correct in a whole series of
cases. However, Yurovsky seemed less keen on the theoretical aspects of
the work, particularly the idea that the law of value was being replaced in
Soviet economy. Instead he believed that the law of value acted everywhere
where there was the market and commodities, even if there were large
organisations of a monopoly type, and even if the state acted to strengthen
or weaken certain economic branches. If the market remained under these
conditions, then the law of value still acted. Preobrazhensky's law of primitive socialist accumulation could alter the conditions in which the law of
value acted, but it did not abolish the law itself.[28]

Yurovsky was also skeptical as to the real nature of the 'law of primitive socialist accumulation'. It was of course possible for the state to accumulate resources for the purposes of socialism using various techniques,
but could this process be called a 'law'? Did this law govern the process of
price formation in the sense of a governing regularity? Yurovsky disputed
that the law of value could be contradicted by the law of primitive socialist
accumulation, since this latter law should really be contrasted to the law of
capitalist accumulation. The question of the logic of accumulation was
separate to the contradiction between the law of value and administrative
methods. The aim of administrative measures could be to accumulate
resources, or it could be (as during the recent civil war) primary socialist
spending of the previous epoch's material resources. The method used to
achieve a certain goal should not be confused with the goal itself.[29]

Moreover, planned regulation of production and distribution implied
for Yurovsky the abolition of free consumption, i.e. the rejection of the
right of consumers to choose which products to consume. If the structure
of demand was to be decided by planners, then consumers could not exercise freedom of choice in this respect. In such a fully planned system only
one regulator would act. Yurovsky stressed that such a regulator was
presently not seen because the form of planning which the state used
aspired to calculate solvent demand, i.e. market demand dependent on
value relations. The existing system should not be understood as of mixed
composition, as a mixture of the past and the future, rather it was a system
of commodity economy containing planned elements. These planned elements did not eliminate commodity economy in any way.[30]

Thus Yurovsky noted that he used the term 'planned economy' in two senses: in the first it meant planning alongside the market, in the second it meant planning that replaced the market. Since Yurovsky believed it was the former type of planning that existed in the Soviet Union he stated that:

> Our economic system is a system of commodity-money economy and planned economy, a planned economy based still on value principles ... do not consider that value principles liquidate industrial or other monopolies. Actually ... the action of the law of value leads to one result in conditions of free competition and another in monopoly.[31]

Yurovsky noted that the Soviet state could, in its capacity as a monopolist, introduce a policy of increasing prices on products made by state enterprises and reducing prices paid by state enterprises. He outlined various goals that the state could pursue in its manipulation of prices, but which ever of the goals was pursued, this would not mean that the law of value was being negated. Regulation of the national economy – so called state intervention – which limited free competition did not oust commodity economy, but only replaced one type by another.

If a capitalist state carried out a policy of stimulating a particular industrial branch by encouraging private capital into it, then the capitalist system remained a commodity economy, and similarly in the Soviet case. Even though such regulation was incomparably greater in the USSR, this did not mean that the law of value no longer acted. Yurovsky accepted that one current goal was socialist accumulation, but how was this policy pursued? It was achieved through a plan to enforce higher prices for state products, higher taxation of commodity turnover and so on, i.e. through markets and prices. For Yurovsky this implied the violation of free competition, but not the ousting of the law of value.[32] Yurovsky thus concluded that Preobrazhensky was incorrect to speak of a struggle between the planning principle and the law of value.

This article showed that Yurovsky was concerned to ensure that equilibrium was restored in the Soviet economy by such means as reducing prices and strict control over currency and credit. It also showed that he believed that the major role of prices was to balance supply and demand on markets, i.e. he had a neoclassical understanding of prices and markets in this respect. As regards the socialist element in the Soviet economy he saw state regulation as this element, although he stressed that this did not mean that the law of value had been overcome. However, since he agreed that the Soviet economy in the 1920s was in a transitional phase, it is clear that this transition had to lead somewhere, but Yurovsky did not clearly outline how he saw the economy developing after the transition phase was over. However, in terms of characterising the Soviet economy generally, Yurovsky employed a more institutionalist view when dissecting its structure, emphasising that elements of planned economy operated within market-control environments in both the Soviet and non-Soviet context.

## V.A. Bazarov and planning methodology

Vladimir Alexandrovich Bazarov (1874–1939) was a highly original theorist of both economics and philosophy and a close personal associate of Bogdanov. One of the editors of a Russian translation of *Capital* that was published in 1907–1909, Bazarov was originally a Bolshevik but had later disassociated himself from their ideas and policies.

Some insightful points were made in relation to planning by Bazarov in an article entitled 'On the Methodology of Constructing Perspective Plans' in 1926. Bazarov stated that perspective plans must unite genetic (current trends) and teleological (future goals) methods of planning, and that the agricultural sector required predominantly genetic planning whereas the state sector required a predominantly teleological approach. He asked the question: what was an optimal plan? His answer contained three conditions. First, that the progress of the economy from the point of departure to the end point indicated by the plan must be smooth and without interruptions, which in turn assumed the existence of sufficient economic reserves. Second, that the economy must be a harmonious, organic whole – a maximally stable system of mobile equilibrium and proportionality. Third, that the path chosen from the initial point to the final goal should be the shortest possible one.[33]

In this article Bazarov also noted some stress points within current Soviet economic policy. Since wages should grow faster than productivity (this presumably being a socialist goal), expenses on reconstruction and growth would be higher than the corresponding norms in capitalist conditions. Since also there were large administrative expenses on the planning apparatus, to achieve the same growth rate observed in advanced capitalist countries in Soviet conditions would be difficult. Bazarov also recognised that his three criteria for optimal planning might contradict each other. In the case of a conflict between the shortest path and proportionality, the latter should prevail. Consequently growth rates might have to be sacrificed to stability. Bazarov also advocated the notion that, except in special cases such as defence needs, the international division of labour should be respected in long-term plans. Despite the abundance of natural resources in the USSR, there would inevitably be:

> individual areas of production in which, owing to natural conditions, we shall be unable in the foreseeable future to bring the cost of production down sufficiently for the domestic product to cost us no more than the foreign output of the same quality. As a general rule output of this type should be left out of the general plan.[34]

This showed that Bazarov partially accepted the rationality of the international division of labour; this clearly contradicted the isolationist policy favoured by Stalin in the 1930s.

## Bazarov's conception of market processes

One of Bazarov's longest and most detailed works from the NEP period was entitled 'The "Curve of Development" of Capitalist and Soviet Economy' which was published in 1926. In this work Bazarov analysed the industrial cycles peculiar to both capitalist and Soviet conditions using thinking analogous to that of the natural sciences.[35]

For example in the natural sciences the precondition of equilibrium was the principle of conservation of energy and materials. A system of economic equilibrium could be interpreted in the form of such a balance, but in terms of social, not physical energy. Bazarov related this to a 'law of market saturation', which he presented as follows. Suppose that on the market there was a definite and stable demand for several different goods that were unavailable. Suppose that the desired commodities then appeared on the market in quantities sufficient for saturating the solvent demand, for example from foreign suppliers. Clearly, the absorption of goods would initially occur especially fast, gradually slowing according to the measure of satisfaction of demand that was achieved.[36] What was the law of this decline? In order to answer this question four preconditions were necessary:

1   that these goods were not replaceable by other goods;
2   that prices did not change;
3   that every consumer acquired one item;
4   that the consumer value of the good was stable.

Given these assumptions, Bazarov stated that the process of market saturation was identical with a chemical reaction with one of the products being removed from the sphere of the reacting liquid. An example was to dissolve sodium carbonate in hydrochloric acid:

$$Na_2CO_3(s) + 2HCl(aq) \rightarrow 2NaCl(aq) + H_2O(l) + CO_2(g)$$

Because carbon dioxide and water were formed from this reaction (commodities, having entered into the sphere of consumption, disappeared from the market), the process went to completion when all molecules of sodium carbonate were transformed into sodium chloride (until full saturation of solvent demand for all consumers was achieved).

Using analogous reasoning, consumers of goods, as opposed to molecules, were endowed with consciousness and will, but their actions were no more diverse than the spontaneous movement of molecules. Therefore with anarchical-market processes, there was no basis to question the statistical regularity required for the theory of solubility. Thus for an analysis of market saturation it was possible to use the category of average probability of collision of a potential purchaser with goods on the market, which was a constant. Giving this the designation p, if A was the number of goods required by purchasers, and x was the number of successful purchases of goods during the period of observation, then the mathematical expectation of the number of purchases in a unit of time was expressed by the formula $p(A - x)$. According to Bazarov this idea expressed the law of market saturation in its simplest form, fully admitting that it rested on many simplifying assumptions.

This analysis shows a number of things. First, that Bazarov was concerned to try to find scientific expressions of the oscillations experienced by capitalism. This involved using assumptions about how the market operated. Second, that Bazarov relied quite heavily on analogous reasoning. Third, although Bazarov was anti-capitalist in his general outlook, he was prepared to engage in academic research concerning capitalist processes and was not content to 'rest on Marx'. This approach was at odds with the Stalinist ideological system that was established in the 1930s. Bazarov's unique conception of market processes had little impact upon actual planning methodology as it developed in the 1930s, but his work demonstrated that conceptual originality in economic theory certainly existed during NEP.

## S.G. Strumilin's view of the function of planning

Stanislav Gustavovich Strumilin (1877–1974) was a key figure in relation to the development of planning methodology in the USSR in the 1920s and beyond. Originally a Menshevik but joining the Bolsheviks in 1923, Lenin himself appointed Strumilin to the staff of Gosplan in 1921. He became a leading figure in developing the economics of planning thereafter, in particular between 1926 and 1929, and he was a central figure in the preparation of the first two drafts of the first five-year plan. At the end of the 1920s Strumilin supported the notion that plans would more likely be realistic if engineers played a major role in creating them.

An insight into Strumilin's understanding of the market in relation to planning can be obtained from a report given at the Fifth Congress of Planning Workers on 8 March 1929 entitled 'Social Problems of the Five-year Plan'. In a section on 'market problems' Strumilin wrote:

> Problems of market equilibrium in conditions of planned economy in current calculation is reduced to projecting such prices for the realisation of the mass of commodities produced under which the demand of wide markets fully covers possible supply.[37]

But market demand was in turn determined by the projected growth of income of the population, i.e. the projected tempo of growth of wages, the rising productivity of agriculture, and a whole series of other factors, which were conditioned by the growth of consumer welfare and the sums taken from individual incomes by taxation. All these elements, which determined the relation of supply to demand, were regulated by the economic plan. Therefore if in a given moment a goods famine was experienced, this demanded to be viewed (according to Strumilin) not as an objective necessity, but as a result of insufficient skill in planning.

Strumilin stated that the basic method of verifying all plans from the point of view of the requirements of market equilibrium was the construction of a provisional balance of supply and demand. This task was 'somewhat complex and theoretically little elaborated', and different departments utilised different methods and thus arrived at different conclusions.[38] For example one table given by Strumilin showed the supply of various industrial goods on the market over a five-year period. This table had two variants shown – a first and an optimal variant. In the first variant (for example) tea supply grew by 272 per cent over the five years, in the optimal variant it grew by 359 per cent; agricultural machinery grew by 372 per cent in the first variant and 432 per cent in the optimal variant. Two things were clear from the manner in which Strumilin presented this data. First, that the question of deciding what particular growth rates to assume and why was not really discussed in such articles. These sort of questions were usually debated 'behind closed doors', and consequently the reasoning proposed to support the various growth rates remained obscure to readers. Second, plans were thus constructed in a rather undemocratic manner. Consultation was usually limited to a narrow group of 'specialists' within and around Bolshevik party institutions such as Gosplan, and little attempt was made to involve the wider population in the planning process.

Perhaps an even more serious consequence of this approach was Strumilin's conception of the market itself as a mechanism for revealing consumer demand, and the idea following on from this that planning should be a replacement for this type of mechanism, i.e. that it must first reveal and then balance consumer requirements. This was to be done not by consulting consumers directly, but through planning estimations of balancing what consumer demand was deemed to be from above. Yurovsky had criticised this approach as restrictive. Strumilin's was a very particular view of what planning should be in relation to a specific view of what the market actually accomplished, one that had important consequences for future developments in the Soviet system. As always, alternatives were available and could have been further developed in detail.

## The end of NEP

Some of the economic ideas just discussed had relevance mainly to the mixed economy of the 1920s, while others had a more general significance, for example with respect to planning after NEP.

NEP itself came to an ignominious end for various interrelated reasons. First, because of a breakdown of the market relation between the government and the peasantry in the winter of 1927/1928 and a subsequent decision to overcome the power of the well-to-do peasants, who were seen as opposing party policy. The idea to allow peasants some market freedom in the early 1920s was in the main forced upon the Bolsheviks, although they had made a virtue out of a necessity. When problems arose in obtaining from peasants the grain that they wanted by market means, the options open to the Bolsheviks for resolving this issue were clear. Second, although NEP was first envisaged 'seriously and for a long time', this period of time was not forever, and at some point planning had to usurp full control away from the market if the classical Marxist prognosis was to be fulfilled. Viewed in this way the ending of NEP was really inevitable, it was just a question of timing. It would certainly have been practically possible of course to continue NEP indefinitely, but this would have meant sacrificing the ideals of industrialisation and planning to some extent at least, and allowing further market-based social differentiation. This would have involved one ideological contortion too far for those absolutely certain in the conviction that their particular interpretation of Marxism was unquestionably true.

## Conclusions

The 1920s were in Russia a period of relative intellectual openness, with competing currents in economics coexisting both in terms of overall approach and concrete specifics. Questions of the role of market-based institutions in a socialist system were articulated and a number of alternative views about how economies in general operated were explored. However towards the end of the 1920s the capacity for relatively free debate gradually faded, as Stalin manoeuvred to take overall control within the Communist Party structure. Over the period 1926 to 1929 the ground-rules for deciding how planning was to operate was to an important extent taken out of the hands of economists and transferred to a party-controlled bureaucracy, which began to stifle any real expressions of dissent. The time for free debates was at an end, instead it was declared to be the time to actually embark upon the full-scale imperative planning of the Soviet economy itself. In the next chapter how this was done will be examined in detail.

# 5 Stalinist economy, 1929–1940

## Key developments in Russia and the West in the 1930s

In Europe and America the 1930s were in part simply a continuation of the fashions and fads of the 1920s, for example the further progression of the *art deco* movement, but they also witnessed some new developments in various important fields of human endeavour. Regarding economic theory, in the UK J.M. Keynes published his avowedly revolutionary *General Theory of Employment, Interest and Money* in 1936, partly as a response to the great depression that followed the Wall Street crash. In this work Keynes pitted himself explicitly against what he characterised as Pigou-type neoclassical orthodoxy, eschewed notions of automatic market-generated equilibrium, and introduced new ideas into economics such as the marginal propensity to save/consume and the liquidity trap. A greater level of state intervention in the economy was the general policy recommendation. In the USA A.A. Berle and G.C. Means published their *Modern Corporation and Private Property* in 1932, a book that placed the faceless corporate system centre stage, with its centralised concentration of power and a separation of ownership from control. Also in the USA Irving Fisher developed his debt-deflation theory of the great depression in which over-indebtedness combined with deflation to produce a prolonged industrial stagnation.

In 1936 the philosopher A.J. Ayer published *Language, Truth and Logic*, where the verification principle required that a statement was meaningful only if some observation was relevant to its truth or falsity. In Germany Hitler declared himself Chancellor of the Reich while Italy invaded Abyssinia in 1935. Niels Bohr's complementarity or Copenhagen interpretation of the formalism of quantum mechanics became established among many physicists. A new type of fibre – nylon – was patented, the *Hindenburg* airship exploded in New York, T.E. Lawrence died in a motorcycle accident and a civil war erupted in Spain.

The USSR in the 1930s was however a very different place to the rest of Europe in the 1930s and also to the USSR in the 1920s. Stalin finally achieved and then consolidated his personal dictatorship into a system of awesome centralised power, which in some ways rivalled that of both Peter the Great and Adolf Hitler. To accomplish this, repression and political purges were the order of the day, with show trials and witch hunts being organised in order to expel so-called dissidents from positions of influence, by tarring them with the brush of being 'bourgeois counter-revolutionaries'. Waves of repression followed by its abatement have been identified through the 1930s, with 1934–1936 experiencing relative success in strictly economic terms. However, the intellectual excitement and achievement of the 1920s was replaced by stale and ominous propaganda of the lowest possible ideational quality. Fear and paranoia permeated many aspects of human activity in the USSR, eventually culminating in the mass slaughter of hundreds of thousands of people between 1936 and 1938. Many leading intellectuals perished in these purges although many others survived, at least in body if not fully in mind. If anti-socialist forces in the West wanted something negative with which to tar socialism, then their wishes could not have been answered more dramatically.

## Soviet economy on the eve of the planning (r)evolution

Out of the debates that raged over the development of the Soviet economy at the very end of the 1920s, the general objectives of industrial growth that were finally established by the ruling party elite have been summarised in four key points as follows:

1   The USSR must overtake the advanced capitalist countries in terms of industrial output per head of the population;
2   The Soviet economy must overtake the West technically;
3   The output of capital goods must increase more rapidly than that of consumer goods;
4   The chosen location of industry should be based on long-term and defence needs rather than short-term factors like costs.[1]

The survival of the USSR in a hostile capitalist world was seen as paramount.

However, these four general goals can be considered to be quite separate from the means by which they were to be accomplished, which was given as centralised imperative planning. The debate over the means by which the four goals were best achieved, that is the alternative systems of economic planning that might have been created to accomplish the said objectives, was something that economists or economic administrators (as opposed to party leaders) should have, and indeed did, contributed the most to resolving. This chapter examines the debates that occurred over planning alternatives in conjunction with the debates that took place over specific planning targets. These two questions are sometimes confused in the academic literature, just as they were (perhaps deliberately so) by some at the time of their occurrence, with the result that the real issues have sometimes not been properly articulated.

Another related question is how far was the actual Soviet system of planning created piecemeal over time – the result of overlaying various new structures of control over existing patterns of behaviour – and how far was it designed on a *tabula rosa*, an original projection of the minds of economists and economic administrators? Both fervent opponents of central planning and those loudly singing its praises claimed that it was a completely new creation, the result of the rational application of Marxist principles to economic management. In reality it is better viewed as the result of thousands of accumulated decisions, both conscious and unconscious, which were taken over many years, together with what remained of patterns of behaviour from many preceding economic institutions and structures, these being partly feudal, partly capitalist and partly proto-socialist in nature. In this sense Soviet planned economy was more an evolutionary development than a revolutionary one. How the various accumulated decisions and behavioural patterns were crystallised into the particular system of planning found in Stalinist economy of the 1930s is the subject of this chapter.

Prior to 1929 various attempts at outlining the operating principles of socialist planning had been made by economists, both within Russia and without. For example within Russia notable attempts had been made by Tugan-Baranovsky in 1917, Krzhizhanovsky through the GOELRO plan in 1920, Kondratiev and Oganovsky in 1924 and Strumilin throughout the 1920s. Other economists such as Brutzkus, Yurovsky and von Mises had forcefully presented many criticisms of possible planning methods, and some of this criticism was even heeded by a few planners. The following sections discuss these pre-1929 conceptions of socialist planning, and ask whether any elements of them were utilised in the methods eventually adopted after 1929, before an account of the development of Stalinist economy itself is provided.

## Tugan-Baranovsky on planning

Perhaps the first attempt at outlining socialist planning techniques in detail from within Russia was made by Tugan-Baranovsky. In *Socialism as a Positive Teaching*, written in the summer of 1917, Tugan-Baranovsky gave a clear indication of how he believed planning should operate, by proceeding from two basic considerations. First planners must calculate the marginal utility of every product, and second they must calculate the labour cost of every product. Thus marginal utility and labour costs were to be seen as the two fundamental elements required for constructing socialist plans.

To give an example, suppose that a rural commune must decide whether to manufacture only goods of primary necessity, or also produce goods the need for which is less compelling. Suppose that the question is whether to produce cucumbers or to limit production to potatoes only. Tugan-Baranovsky proposed that the schematisation of the need for potatoes and cucumbers should be presented according to the method of the Austrian economist Carl Menger:

| Potatoes | Cucumbers |
| --- | --- |
| 9 | 4 |
| 8 | 3 |
| 7 | 2 |
| 6 | 1 |
| 5 | 0 |
| 4 | |
| 3 | |
| 2 | |
| 1 | |
| 0 | |

The utility of the first unit of potato to a consumer was expressed as 9, the utility of the first unit of cucumber as 4. The utility of each subsequent unit of potato and cucumber declined as the desire for them became satiated, eventually reaching zero, the state of full satisfaction. Tugan-Baranovsky then supposed that the labour cost of producing a unit of potato was twice that of producing a unit of cucumber, and that the commune had at its disposal 4 units of labour. In this example no cucumbers would be produced, as total utility was maximised by producing 4 units of potatoes $(9 + 8 + 7 + 6 = 30)$. Producing one unit of cucumber resulted in total utility of only 21 $(9 + 8 + 4)$.[2]

But suppose instead that 10 units of labour were available. In this case total utility would be maximised by producing 8 units of potatoes and 1 unit of cucumber $(9 + 8 + 7 + 6 + 5 + 4 + 3 + 2 + 4 = 48)$. If only potatoes were produced then total utility would be 45 $(9 + 8 + 7 + 6 + 5 + 4 + 3 + 2 + 1 + 0)$, and if 2 units of cucumber were produced then total utility would be 46 $(9 + 8 + 7 + 6 + 5 + 4 + 4 + 3)$. Tugan-Baranovsky concluded that it was thus clear how economic plans should be constructed in socialism, by using the marginal utility of every product together with its labour cost of production. He summarised the method as follows:

> With the composition of the economic plan socialist society will aspire to distribute social labour between various types of production, in order that the marginal utility of the products produced would be proportional to their labour cost ... Under this distribution of social labour maximum social benefit is achieved.[3]

This is perhaps the first reference in Russian economics to the idea of an optimal plan, an idea that was later made famous by L.V. Kantorovich.

Regarding the international component of planned economy, Tugan-Baranovsky conceived of global socialism as a system of equal sovereign states, with citizens of all states having the right to move from one state to another without hindrance. States would not attempt to gain an advantage over each other by means of trade policy, as all tariff barriers would be abolished and the advantages of the international division of labour would be allowed to develop fully:

> the socialist state will not have the motive of artificially developing in its country one branch of industry on account of another similar state, since the socialist state will not fear other states ... the international economic policy of the socialist state must have a very different direction than the current situation, and should aim at the greatest use of natural productive forces and all the economic advantages of its country.[4]

Individual states under socialism would relate to each other as members of one political family. In one state industry would predominate, in another agriculture, but this would not be a danger, as the possibility of states exploiting each other would have faded. This view of what the international socialist economy should be was very different to the isolationism and forced industrialisation promoted by Stalin after 1929, although so were the circumstances in which they were engendered, the prospects for international revolution having faded.

Tugan-Baranovsky's effort had very little influence on early Bolshevik attempts at planning, which at least initially took a rather different non-economic or quasi-engineering approach to the problem of plan design, in line with idea that developing the socialist economy was more a technical task than a theoretical one. For example a Committee for Utilisation was created in November 1918, the function of which was to calculate the total demand for products and the amounts available for supply, and specific plans were composed relating to norms of consumption for various food products.[5] However the idea of calculating the marginal utility and labour costs of such products was not explicitly mentioned. The quasi-engineering approach to planning held by many Bolsheviks was epitomised in the GOELRO plan, discussed in detail later in this chapter, but it also found echoes across in Atlantic in the work of Thorstein Veblen.

## Veblen's Soviet of technicians

After 1917 Russian economists were not the only people considering how to replace market-control systems with other more transparent forms of economic planning. In America Thorstein Veblen had in 1919 proposed the notion of a 'Soviet of technicians', the terminology itself giving a clue to the fact that Veblen had perhaps taken a cue from his Russian counterparts. After the insidious vested interests of the American industrial order had finally been overturned, Veblen suggested that a plan of concerted action should:

> engage the intelligent cooperation of several thousand technically trained men scattered over the face of the country, in one industry and another; must carry out a passably complete cadastration of the country's industrial forces; must set up practicable organization tables covering the country's industry in some detail – energy resources, materials and man power; and it must also engage the aggressive support of the trained men at work in transportation, mining, and the greater mechanical industries.[6]

Veblen believed that the duties of the incoming directorate would be in the main of a technological nature, and be designed to correct the shortcomings of the old industrial order in relation to the allocation of resources, the avoidance of waste and the supply of goods and services. What Veblen termed 'consulting economists' would be a necessary adjunct to the work of the central directorate, playing a role analogous to the part played by legal council in diplomatic manoeuvres. However Veblen had little hope that a revolutionary overthrow of the vested interests in America would actually occur, and hence his Soviet of technicians was more an exercise in a longed for 'what if' rather than a resolute 'when'. Even so the similarity with developments in post-revolutionary Russia was unlikely to have been completely accidental.

## The GOELRO plan

The idea of the GOELRO plan was first presented in February 1920, the driving force behind the commission set up to implement it being the electrical engineer G.M. Krzhizhanovsky. Its central goal was the electrification of Russia, or the establishment of network of electric power stations for industry, agriculture and transport. Lenin was particularly enthusiastic about this idea, and GOELRO has been labelled (perhaps unrealistically) as the first imperative economic plan ever composed and then implemented in human history.

Lenin had published an article on 21 February 1921 entitled 'An Integrated Economic Plan' in which he extolled the virtues of the GOELRO endeavour, describing it as a 'first-class' effort. Over 180 specialists had worked on it, the best talent available, and it had provided the locations of the first twenty steam power and ten water power electric stations, together with a description of the economic importance of each. Lenin wrote:

The plan ranges over about ten years and gives an indication of the number of workers and capacities (in 1000 hp) ... We have precise calculations by experts for every major item, and every industry. To give a small example, we have their calculations for the output of leather, footwear at two pairs a head (300 million pairs) etc. As a result we have a material and a financial (gold rubles) balance-sheet for electrification (about 370 million working days, so many barrels of cement, so many bricks, poods of iron, copper ...). It envisages ... an 80 per cent increase in manufacturing, and 80–100 per cent in extracting industry over the next ten years. The gold balance deficit (... about 6 billion) 'can be covered by means of concessions and credit operations'.[7]

GOELRO also provided an estimate for each year from 1921 to 1930 of the number of power stations that could be run in and the degree to which the existing ones could be enlarged. Various specific targets were given in terms of production goals for ten or fifteen years in the future as follows. The production of pig iron was to grow from 4.2 million tons in 1913 to 8.2 million, iron ore from 9.2 million tons to 19.6 million, cement from 1.5 million tons to 7.75 million, and coal from 29.1 million tons to 62.3 million. Total investment was provided at 17 billion rubles.[8]

In the article on GOELRO, Lenin was particularly disdainful of 'empty talk and word-spinning' with respects to debates over planning, which he believed was in danger of replacing the painstaking and thoughtful study of practical experience which was really required. The role of technical specialists was seen as crucial. Lenin opined that 'the efficient economist, instead of penning empty phrases, will get down to a study of the facts and figures, and analyse our own practical experience.'[9] However the fact that Lenin used the term 'economist' rather than 'planner' was revealing; he was by 1921 losing patience with conceited Communists and bureaucratic complacency, in which (it was implied) he foresaw the possible downfall of the USSR.

In terms of results, the GOELRO plan has been subject to very different evaluations. Lenin reported at one point that by December 1921, 221 electrical stations had been opened across the country in the previous two years, implying that GOELRO was a great success. Jasny however took a different view, stating that the effect of GOELRO on developments in the Russian economy was very close to zero.[10] Zaleski suggested that many of the specific production targets were indeed fulfilled over a period of between ten and fifteen years, but at a much greater cost than had initially been foreseen. As mentioned earlier, perhaps the GOELRO plan's most significant legacy was the narrowly technical and empiricist conception of planning that it embodied. However, at a more fundamental level it is relevant to ask, how had the methodology of construction of the GOELRO plan been elaborated, and what was the connection between building electrical power stations and constructing socialist forms of economy? In fact the question of planning methodology had been little considered before the GOELRO plan itself was developed, and it was assumed without much debate that a directive plan would be an appropriate way to construct new sources of energy.

## The creation and function of Gosplan

On 22 February 1921 SNK proposed a 'general state planning commission' and on 17 March 1921 it issued a decree entitled 'On a Planning Commission'. The practical fulfilment of plans established by the Planning Commission was to be accomplished through the organs of the corresponding People's Commissariats.[11] Various published works foreshadowed the creation of Gosplan, works such as 'A Single Economic Plan and a Single Economic Apparatus' of 1920 by S.I. Gusev. In A.M. Kaktyn's 'A Single Economic Plan and a Single Economic Centre', also of 1920, the creation of a unified, strong-willed, centralised planning unit was posited as the cardinal condition for the existence of a socialistic system of production and exchange.[12]

The basic task of Gosplan was given as to compose a single unified plan for the entire Soviet economy, including means for implementation and fulfilment, and to bring into balance the draft projections of the various different control organs such as the individual People's Commissariats and the federal republics. In 1923 300 people were employed by Gosplan, by 1934 this number had in one estimate risen to 425 (excluding statisticians), of which 150 were managers, 67 were engineers, 13 were agronomists and 142 were economists.[13] It is likely however that the real number of employees was higher than this when regional departments were included in the calculation. In the 1920s Gosplan was led by first class economists such as V.G. Groman and S.G. Strumilin, but by the end of the 1920s many of the pioneers of the planning debates which took place during NEP had been purged and replaced by less illustrious figures. By the end of the 1930s the idea that Gosplan should directly and uncritically follow Communist Party directives was established in Stalinist ideology, although behind the facade some disputes no doubt still occurred.

It is worth pointing out that the function of Gosplan developed primarily as planning itself developed, and that the debates over planning methodology occurred directly alongside concrete attempts to draft specific plans. Why this is important is that the precise role of Soviet planning agencies could have been formed by various alternative paths, for example by allocating a specified period of time (say five years) in which the role and methodology of planning was discussed in detail, without attempting to have any specific planning influence on the actual economy at all. Only when many of the methodological problems were solved would the creation of an actual plan then been attempted. But because the fact that the

Bolsheviks had taken control of Russia was something of a surprise even to them, they had no detailed idea as to how planning would actually function, and chose (some would say were forced) to develop planning methodology and institutions in tandem with promoting particular examples of plans themselves. It is certainly possible to conceive of alternatives to this particular route, but which of course would not necessarily guarantee a greater degree of success.

While many of the economic institutions of the NEP system continued to operate in the 1930s, the character and influence of many of them changed. For example Gosplan grew in stature and importance as planning itself became more prevalent, although higher bodies such as the Politburo still exerted a powerful influence over it. Some commissariat reforms were also undertaken, for example NKVnuVneshTorg was divided into separate Commissariats of Internal Trade (NKVnuTorg) and Foreign Trade (NKVneshTorg), the former then becoming the Commissariat of Supply (NKSnab). In general individual commissariats had power and influence in part in proportion to the status of their commander-in-chief, the People's Commissar, but also in relation to the importance of the sector of the economy that they controlled. As the Soviet planning institutions grew up over time, their history (and pre-history) played an important part in determining their structure. But their underlying nature was inevitably determined by mental conceptions of how planning should operate, i.e. by ideas first and foremost, and such ideas were always held and propagated by individuals, albeit in a group-based environment.

## Kondratiev's plan for agriculture and forestry, 1924–1928

It is worth examining examples of plans that were created by those outside of immediate Bolshevik influence. One of the earliest attempts at concrete plan creation was Kondratiev's plan for agriculture and forestry, 1924–1928, prepared by Kondratiev and various co-workers from within NKZem. While this was a plan designed only for one sector of the economy, since agriculture was such an important part of overall Russian output, Kondratiev's plan had great significance. Work began on this plan in June 1922, the final draft not being completed until July 1925 amidst much controversy. Dispute focused both on the methodology that was employed and on the specific targets that were presented. Kondratiev favoured a planning methodology that gave serious consideration to both past regularities and to the current position of agriculture, before going on to propose realistic targets for the future based partly on extrapolation. In consequence the resultant plan was accused by critics of being too timid, of giving too much weight to the existing structure of agriculture, rather than boldly decreeing the instantaneous transformation to the socialist future.

In general terms Kondratiev's plan envisaged the strengthening of intensive cattle-rearing, declining extensive farming in some regions against increasing extensive farming in other regions, the intensification of certain branches such as fodder crops, and the differentiation and development of the division of labour between regions within Russia. In specific terms the plan projected an increase in total crop sown area of from 36 per cent to 47 per cent between 1923 and 1928, depending on which draft was consulted, and of either 28 per cent or 41 per cent for the growth of livestock levels for the same period. In relation to fulfilment Kondratiev's plan was in the event mildly over-fulfilled in certain areas, although not significantly so, but this fact was seized upon by critics to suggest that Kondratiev's planning methodology was not particularly socialist.

## The balance of the national economy

Another important invention of the NEP period with important ramifications for the planning process was the balance of the national economy prepared by Popov from within TsSU and published fully in the middle of 1926. A 'chessboard-style' table of turnover figures for branches of Russian industry had appeared in a balance of the national economy prepared between 1923–1924. This was a precursor to Leontief-type input-output analysis and was devoted to tracing the sectoral interrelations making up the economy, an important feature to comprehend if planning was to be conducted successfully. Input-output analysis came to describe the flow of goods and services amongst various sectors of an economy in detail, an idea first developed by Francois Quesnay in 1758, although the Soviet effort was certainly an important marker along the way. Other precursors could be seen as Marx (his reproduction schemes), Dmitriev (an equation relating labour inputs expended on production) and the pre-war Russian grain balances prepared by *zemstvo* statisticians.

Popov's balance of the national economy attempted to provide a *post-factum* account of the whole process of the currently existing connections of production and consumption in the economy, i.e. both manufacture and distribution measured in terms of a statistical census, as a prerequisite to the attempt at creating prognostic plans. The eponymous idea of a 'balance' signified that the interrelations between the elements of the economy were seen as paramount, which further implied that development considered without due respect for such balance would be flawed. Popov's concern that detailed statistical accounts of the existing structure of the Russian economy were an essential prerequisite for creating plans was eventually overridden by those with a different conception of how planning should operate, one that favoured specific sectoral plans coordinated homogeneously by the centre. However, Popov's balance was still an important achievement in the continuing development of Russian economics.

## The control figures

Before the fully-fledged five-year plans of 1929–1933 and after were born, a partial precursor to them existed called the annual control figures, which began to be issued in 1925/1926. Although the control figures existed side by side with budgets and financial plans, they were a preliminary attempt by Gosplan to develop the techniques of imperative planning. Perhaps the most important economist responsible for their creation was V.G. Groman, who also worked in detail on analysing the 'laws of recovery' that were operating in the Soviet economy. The aim of the Gosplan control figures was to navigate the proportional crises-free development of the most important branches of the national economy, namely agriculture and industry, and to express in the form of planned estimates all the manifestations of the economic life of the country that were subject to government control. They were initially intended more as a prediction of future economic performance rather than a directive that was set in stone, and thus they did not have the operative force that the later five-year plans would have.

After their first publication for the fiscal year 1925/1926 the control figures were criticised from both wings, by VSNKh for positing an insufficiently rapid rate of development for industry, and by NKZem for giving inadequate attention to the interests of agriculture, suggesting that Gosplan was initially quite cautious about the scope of its work. However, if the published control figures for 1925/1926 consisted of a less than 100 page document, then by 1927/1928 the control figures had expanded to 600 pages, indicating both the growing importance of central planning as an intended mechanism of control and the increased confidence of Gosplan as a planning agency. The control figures for 1927/1928 had compulsory status, which meant that all enterprises and agencies had to take account of them when planning their own activities. Overall they marked an important stepping-stone to the fully comprehensive system of plans begun in 1929.

## The first five-year plan, 1929–1933

The initial burst of enthusiasm for hugely optimistic plan targets in the period 1929–1931 has subsequently been labelled as 'Bacchanalian planning'. While it is to be doubted that much sensual pleasure was obtained through the process of central planning in this period, the picture of frenzied abandon to the logic of constantly raised targets aptly captures the mood of the time. The conception of central planning that dominated at this time was aptly summarised in the following quotation:

> In the process of implementing the five-year plan we physically feel with all the fibres of our being how much we need to organise a social and political mechanism enabling 150 million people to act guided by

a single will, a single striving to accomplish what is laid down in the plan.[14]

Whose 'single will' was to be followed was not made explicit, but implicitly it was that of the Communist Party and ultimately Comrade Stalin. Why the five-year plan had to follow a 'single will', and not be driven by the expression of many democratically amalgamated wills, was not ever specified in detail.

Preparatory work for a long-term plan began seriously in mid-1927 with a decree from SNK calling for a single all-union plan facilitating specialisation and industrialisation. As noted previously the Gosplan economist Strumilin played a major role in drawing up the initial drafts of the first five-year plan, but he soon became sidelined as more ambitious targets were proposed. For example by the summer of 1929 a series of upward revisions to previous plan targets occurred with respect to some key industrial branches. Pig iron production, which had reached an actual level of 3.3 million tons in 1927/1928, was projected to grow to 9 million tons in 1932/1933 in a basic variant of the plan, to 10 million tons in an optimal variant, and to as much as 16.4 million tons in a December 1929 version of the plan. A target of 17 million tons was finally adopted at the Sixteenth Party Congress in July 1930, but not before a figure of 25 million tons had been first mentioned.[15] The target of 17 million tons of pig iron for 1932/1933 represented an increase of more than five times the 1927/1928 base level figure, an extraordinary projected rate of growth for a five-year period. A key element of planned industrialisation one level up would soon turn out to be the planning of capital investment targets that had a knock-on effect in each sector to which they applied, for example investment in iron and steel production, which was then used to make specific pieces of equipment, tractors and so on.

Campaigns to encourage what was called 'socialist emulation' among the industrial workforce were used to increase labour productivity in the first five-year plan starting in 1929–1930. This emulation miraculously transformed the heavy and monotonous burden of labour (as it was seen in capitalism) into a matter of glory and heroic achievement under socialism, simply by positing that the work was being undertaken in the interests of all. From a very different perspective socialist emulation could be viewed as a deceitful trick to encourage certain groups of people to work harder, so that other more cunning and devious groups might benefit.

On completion of the first five-year plan there were certainly major advances achieved in the Soviet economy in relation to physical output. Hundreds of mining, engineering and metallurgical enterprises had begun production, the Magnitogorsk combine was created for the manufacture of iron and steel virtually out of nothing, and new turbines had begun operation in Dneprostroi. Such large increases in productive capacity were heralded as indicators of the success of the first five-year plan, but the question of how the new industries constituted socialist institutions in terms of their organisational structure was discussed much less than the outright volume of production that was achieved. Quantitative rather than qualitative measures were at this time the order of the day. However the system of all-encompassing planning was certainly not fully comprehensive at this time, as in the spring of 1932 some market and semi-market features had been introduced into the Soviet economic system. For example so-called commercial prices and commercial trade were allowed to exist alongside prices fixed by the state. Thus even at the height of enthusiasm for imperative planning, market forms of economy could still be found to exist in some areas of the Soviet system.

## The second five-year plan, 1933–1937

A 'storming' mentality at least initially drove the process of drafting the second five-year plan, but this soon gave way to more modest targets as a crisis involving rationing and inflation took hold in the Soviet economy in 1932–1933. In a party directive from the very beginning of 1932 for example, the basic task of the second five-year plan was given as the reconstruction of the entire national economy and the creation of a new technical base for all the branches of it. In the directive machine construction was projected to increase by 3 to 3.5 times in 1937 as against the level of 1932, the mining of coal was to grow from 90 million tons to 250 million in 1937, the construction of 25–30,000 kilometres of new railway lines would take place, and 22 million ton of cast iron would be smelted in the final year of the plan.[16] However, by the beginning of 1934, the very optimistic targets given in 1932 had been reduced significantly, and total production of all industry was set at 92.7 billion rubles in 1937 as against 43 billion at the start of the plan, a rather more modest increase overall of 2.1 times or a yearly rate of growth of 16.5 per cent.[17]

Social objectives such as the improvement of both rural and urban living conditions and the elimination of social classes were important general objectives of the second five-year plan. The average money wage for workers and employees was projected to grow from 1427 rubles per year in 1932, to 1755 rubles per year in 1937, a rather modest increase of only 23 per cent. However a more rapid growth in the production of consumer goods as against producer goods was at least planned, even if this target was not fulfilled entirely. Consumer goods' production was projected to grow from 20.2 billion rubles in 1932 to 47.2 billion in 1937, but this plan was only 85.4 per cent fulfilled. This suggested that while some planners realised in theory that Soviet economy was deficient in catering to consumer needs at this time, they found it difficult to remedy this fact through practical planning techniques.

The second five-year plan also witnessed the birth of the Stakhanovite movement, devoted to producing record output levels through a large and enthusiastically generated increase in the intensity of work in various sectors of the economy such as coal mining. However, while some impressive new targets were in fact achieved, Stakhanovite methods sometimes resulted in breakdowns, defective goods and the deterioration of equipment due to a lack of repairs, suggesting that it might have been a false economy at least in some instances. Moreover wasn't socialism supposed to be about reducing the burden of labour for ordinary workers rather than increasing it? Under the first two five-year plans a number of very large industrial undertakings intended to emulate US large-scale projects were completed, for example a Turkestan-Siberian railway, the Stalingrad and Kharkhov tractor factories, and steel plants at Magnitogorsk. But by the end of 1937 and the beginning of 1938, the flawed conception of both such 'gigantomania' and also Stakhanovism came to be recognised by some party leaders such as L.M. Kaganovich.[18] This suggests that sometimes at least, the long-term rationality of Soviet economic plans were subordinated to abruptly changing short-term political considerations.

## The third five-year plan, 1938–1942

During the drafting of the third five-year plan a process of purging the party of allegedly counter-revolutionary elements had begun in Soviet society, a process that affected Gosplan directly. As a result Nikolai Voznesensky became head of Gosplan in January 1938, and the further rapid development of heavy industry was envisaged. The third five-year plan was also affected by preparations for a possible war.

Overall the plan projected a significant increase in national income – by 80 per cent by 1942 – and a large rise in gross industrial production – by 92 per cent by 1942. However the average money wage of workers and employees was to grow by only 37 per cent over five years, and the portion of consumption in total national income was to be less in 1942 that it was in 1937. Zaleski described the plan as one of great austerity. Perhaps this was partly so due to the looming shadow of war, and since goals for labour productivity were set quite high – an average increase of 65 per cent over five years – no slackening was to be allowed in the further development of labour discipline. The third five-year plan was of course disrupted by the outbreak of war in 1940, although a concerted effort to preserve many of the initial goals of the plan was made.

## The results achieved by Stalinist economy

Figures vary widely for the actual annual rate of growth of Soviet industry that was achieved between 1929 and 1940. Some official Soviet figures claimed an annual rate as high as 21.7 per cent, whilst some more conservative Western estimates put the figure at 7.1 per cent.[19] Even this lower figure is certainly impressive in itself, especially when compared with many Western economies that were in depression in the 1930s, but it does not give much indication of the quality of products that were manufactured or of changes to labour productivity. New industries such as armaments and agricultural machinery had been established in the USSR virtually from scratch, together with significant improvements in those industries making their raw material inputs such as iron and steel, but progress in the manufacture of consumer goods was much less significant. Important demographic changes also occurred, with large-scale factories absorbing workers from declining small-scale manufacture. The fact that the production of capital goods received significant priority had led to some spectacular technical achievements, but as those victims of the 1932–1933 famine in the Ukraine might attest, human beings cannot eat iron and steel.

What of the more intangible elements of Stalinist economy? Were the new forms of socialist economy created in the 1930s clearly less exploitative than their capitalist counterparts? As might be expected, it all depends on how you interpret the term exploitation. The living conditions of most Soviet workers actually declined in the first half of the 1930s, with poor housing, falling real wages and inadequate diet being common, but on the other hand some public services such as education and health provision improved. It is very likely true that some workers at least genuinely believed in the idea that they were working for the socialist future, and hence their state of mind in the workplace might well have been more positive than it was in Tsarist times. Whether ordinary people in fact had more control over their daily work activities than they did in capitalist forms of economy might be disputed, but they were probably a little happier than (at minimum) their unemployed counterparts in the USA at this time.

## Alternatives to the first three five-year plans

The idea of alternatives to the first three five-year plans might appear at first sight to be relatively straightforward to consider, as Gosplan had actually prepared variant drafts of the individual plans itself. In this sense planners had actually considered various economic possibilities themselves, and various choices had been selected. However, as the problem of evaluating fulfilment levels demonstrated, plans were often being revised as they were actually in progress, suggesting that an iteration process of constant adjustment to reality frequently occurred. Thus, rather than consider various alternatives to specific planning targets, which themselves were often contested terrain, it is perhaps more fruitful to first consider alternatives to the overall system and methodology of planning adopted in the 1930s, and alternatives to the institutions designed to construct and regulate planning activities.

One important element to consider was, to what extent could plans have been constructed with more allowance for democratic input from ordinary citizens. The overall goals of each plan were usually set at the highest possible level, and increased consultation in this aspect was at least possible to conceive of in theory. When considering lower levels of plan construction, such as commissariat disaggregation of targets given to them from above, increased consumer participation was again possible to consider. In a more radical view, the system of planning itself could have been the partial result of more democratic mechanisms of decision-making, with various options being tested and then chosen by referendum or by individual candidate selection. Moreover the political system could have been democratically connected to the planning process, with planners themselves subject to fixed terms in office which were then subject to electoral challenge. Election campaigns with those supporting one type of planning against another could have been fought, the ballot box providing the final answer. Such options might sound unrealistic given the actual situation in the USSR, but are worth considering as points of reference for the politically stunted reality that did unfold.

Holland Hunter and Janusz Szyrmer have provided an econometric test of various alternative strategies for the economic development of the USSR in the 1930s. Using the balance of the Soviet economy prepared in 1932 as a framework, they calculated the impact of hypothetical changes in specific policy variables on Soviet economic performance to 1941, for example changes to variables such as population growth, defence outlays, livestock consumption and factor productivity. They concluded that if Soviet exports and imports had grown by 20 per cent per annum after 1928, the favourable impact on the level of capital by 1941 would have been 4 billion rubles. Moreover if collectivisation had been avoided and with changes to some other variables involved, an additional level of between 34 and 46 billion rubles of fixed capital could have been available in 1941.[20] This calculation suggested that even within the planning framework that was then in existence, improvements to the specific results that were advocated could have been made by means of alternative policies.

## The temporal span of plans

Three basic types of plan existed in the USSR in the 1930s – quarterly, yearly and five-year plans. In theory four quarterly plans should match a yearly plan and five yearly plans a five-year plan but this was not always the case. Plans were constantly modified as reality itself unfolded, both before and after particular plans were supposed to become operative, and hence the various different plans did not always fully harmonise after they were finally completed. In some ways the quarterly and yearly plans were supposed to make operative what had been outlined in the five-year plan, but in other cases direct conflict between the various plans could be found.

The procedure for drafting the annual plans encompassed four stages. The first was drafting a limited number of indexes, the second was completing an entire draft, the third was arbitration in relation to different parts of the plan, and the fourth was obtaining final approval of the plan, although these stages did not always operate as envisaged. Thus plans for constructing plans were subject to continual revision. Taking a specific example – the second five-year plan (1933–1937) and the yearly plans for the same period in relation to the food industry – yearly plans were generally more realistic than the yearly expressions of the five-year plan, and consequently were more likely to be fulfilled. This was partly due to the fact that, especially by the time of the later years of a five-year plan, reality itself could better be expressed in the yearly plans, since closer temporal proximity was possible.

The five-year plans became the most well known examples of Stalinist economy, at least outside the USSR, but it might be asked why a span of five years was chosen as the norm. Why not three or eight years? Was there something especially socialistic about this length of time that assisted in the planning process? The answer of course was no, there was not, but five years became the standard planning time horizon through a process of trial and error. It seemed an appropriate period of time to consider in relation to the cycle of industrial investments and other fluctuations, and also with respect to the period of construction of large projects such as power stations and railway lines. In regards to this specific question (as in many others), the system of planning had been made subordinate to the goals of industrialisation. That not everyone agreed that this timescale was appropriate was evident from W.A. Lewis's warning that a general five-year plan for a whole national economy was no more than a game, as five years was too far ahead to see exactly what could be happening in areas such as domestic productivity and the international terms of trade.[21]

## Features of the Soviet planning system in the 1930s

It has been argued by some that at this time a coherent planning system did not actually exist in the USSR and that Gosplan was only a subordinate agency of the Poliburo, political motivations actually dominating everything. It is true that the Soviet system of planning was coming into being throughout the 1930s, but some key and essential features were indeed present at this time. For example the need for uniform plan indicators to establish coherence across the entire system was established in the early 1930s, something that was obviously essential if numerical targets were to be followed to the last decimal place. Another area of developing interest was in relation to determining consumer requirements.

In the USSR in the mid-1930s some apparently genuine attempts at divining consumer demand were in fact made. Various methods for this such as preliminary orders, open questionnaires, illustrated catalogues and displays, comment books, the organisation of exhibitions, and consumer conferences were discussed in Soviet journals.[22] These techniques were

designed to gauge the level and structure of consumer demand for products that were being considered for manufacture. However, the nature of
the response from consumers which was being elicited was very basic,
being simply whether a new good might be desired or not, and if so how
much of it was required.

For example one Soviet commentator explained that between 1932 and
1934 various exhibitions of goods to be manufactured by Soviet light
industry took place. The technique used for revealing demand was that
every exhibited model, specimen, and fashion was measured for 'satisfaction'. Visitors to the exhibition received questionnaires in which they were
asked to indicate those products that they thought most desirable. After
the exhibition, producers calculated which products were most positively
received, and these were then put into production. Those products that
provoked negative reactions were either not produced or the level of their
production was reduced. For example at exhibitions of the cotton fibre
industry, the results of the surveys conducted suggested that consumers in
different regions had varied tastes. Patterned flannel was popular in
Nal'chik, but far less so in Gorky and Moscow, while satin was successful
in Moscow and Gorky yet shunned in Nal'chik.[23] Such consultation was
not a general feature of Stalinist planning.

## Decision-making in the planning system

As a specific example of a more general process, it is worth examining the
decision-making process with regards to economic planning in more detail,
for example in relation to food supply and internal trade. In 1930 the
People's Commissariat of Supply became responsible for internal trade
matters (shops and eating establishments) and also for the food industry,
then in 1934 this dual function was split into two separate People's Commissariats. Consequently the People's Commissariat of Internal Trade was
divided into 14 departments and various chief administrations, and it was
responsible for the detailed drafting of plans relevant to internal trade.
However separate functional committees such as the Price Committee
(attached to the Council of Labour and Defence) held important powers
with respect to trade affairs, powers such as price fixing and ensuring plan
fulfillment, and hence individual People's Commissariats operated in an
environment of complex inter-institutional overlap.

In relation to planning population consumption norms, in the early
1930s physiological data was used from various sources, together with
comparison with standards in the USA, in order to gauge the levels
required. Theoretically at least such fixed consumption norms for each
individual could then be used to generate specific planning targets for production and investment levels, in tandem with projected population
growth, this being a demand-side approach to the planning of food
production. However, inter-commissariat conflict often occurred in the

planning process and hence such a demand-side approach was unlikely to have been used without additional factors also coming into play.

Drafting of the five-year plans themselves was, for the Supply Commissariats, a very protracted process. For the second five-year plan it started with general aims set from above (the Politburo), these then were cast into basic indicators by the plan bureau of the Supply Commissariat, a first draft of the whole plan for trade was then produced, this was then subject to a whole series of inputs and changes from within and without the Commissariat, revisions and a new draft were subsequently produced, and so on a number of times until the higher authorities were satisfied with the final result. This process of revision even continued after the plan was supposed to come into operation.

Moreover, inter-institutional overlap also occurred in trade affairs with regards to the Council of People's Commissars and the Council of Labour and Defence's influence on planning with respect to the People's Commissariat of Supply, both whilst plans were being drafted and also whilst being implemented. The Council of People's Commissars sometimes issued decrees on grain delivery, fulfilment progress and plan disaggregation, orders that the Commissariat itself was obliged to take very seriously. Within the trade Commissariats themselves, intra-institutional conflicts also arose, for example regional branches of the Commissariat of Supply sometimes approached the central all-union body for a redistribution of pre-allocated resources. In general decision-making in relation to Commissariat planning targets in the 1930s occurred at least in part according to political criteria, and together with imperfect knowledge and continuing shifts in the balance of power between institutions and individuals, this made for a continually evolving network of decision-making patterns. This type of system complexity is of course common to many organisational structures, not just Soviet-style economic planning.

## An optimal plan

Enough experience had been accumulated by the end of the 1930s to begin to see obvious flaws in some planning techniques, even if such insights contradicted Marxist teachings. For example the idea of an optimal plan was first suggested by the economist L.V. Kantorovich in a work first published in Leningrad in 1939, an idea that later contributed to his receiving the Nobel Prize in economics. The idea of an economic optimum had been negatively associated with neoclassical economics in the minds of most Bolsheviks. The 1939 study initially proposed a method for solving various technical problems such as the least wasteful allocation of work to machines and the shaping of materials with minimum loss, but Kantorovich soon realised that the method outlined had more general application to the planning process. Kantorovich explicitly acknowledged that deficiencies in Soviet planning procedures existed, due to the fact that economic science lagged behind the requirements of a socialist system, and also that existing plans were not necessarily fully efficient.

The notion of an optimal plan that Kantorovich proposed to rectify this was a plan in which the proposed product assortment was optimally distributed amongst firms at the lowest possible cost of production. Within the optimal plan the principle of profitability was observed, that is each factory was assigned the production of that type of good on which it had the highest net product.[24] Using a system of so-called objectively determined valuations and economic indices, in which resources were categorised with respect to their scarcity, Kantorovich devised specific methods for ensuring the maximum fulfilment of the programme task in terms of the given assortment of goods.

However, the notion of an optimal plan could be criticised for simply mimicking techniques that were supposedly employed naturally in market-control systems, in order to achieve the most rational allocation of goods. That it had become politically acceptable in the USSR to (by implication) make this suggestion in the early 1940s suggests that the Soviet leadership had become more comfortable with their long-term survival prospects. Tugan-Baranovsky had made a similar suggestion in 1917 through the concept of marginal planning, but had been vigorously castigated by Lenin as a 'bourgeois ideologue'. Fashions and fads clearly played a role in the Soviet economic system just as they did in its nemesis in the West.

## Socialist agricultural and industrial formations

The question of the collectivisation of agriculture was a crucial one both before 1929 and after this date. The decision to collectivise agriculture was taken for a number of reasons – to try to increase the available grain surplus, to rationalise and mechanise agriculture, to promote socialist economic formations in Soviet society, and to quell the nascent power of the well-to-do peasants. However the particular nature of the form of collectivisation actually implemented is pertinent to understanding the type of socialist institutions that were created in the 1930s. In a central committee decree from June 1929 entitled 'On the organisational construction of agricultural cooperation', various tasks were outlined with regards to the socialist reconstruction of the countryside as follows:

1   the organisation of a special system of agricultural cooperation on the basis of branches of production for every region;
2   the introduction of basic levers for the reconstruction of agriculture such as producer credit, the supply of tools and machinery, the supply of seeds and so on;
3   the development on a contractual basis of a mass form of productive cooperative farms and large-scale collective farms;
4   the restructuring of agricultural credit;

5    the strengthening of the leadership of cooperatives in relation to party
      and Soviet management organs.[25]

This last task demonstrated that control of the new cooperatives would
from the start be in the hands of the party and state bureaucracy.

Wheatcroft and Davies related that at first the Soviet authorities aimed
for the socialisation and the rationalisation/mechanisation of agriculture in
tandem, but when this proved difficult they opted for the bringing together
of peasant tools of production in collective farms without mechanisation.
Moreover policies regarding collective farm structure were improvised and
often altered between 1929 and 1932, and were usually designed by those
who lacked much experience of farming.[26] That the collectivisation process
was a failure in terms of encouraging peasants to produce more is thus
understandable, and suggests that the apparently socialist nature of Soviet
collective farms should not always be taken at face value. The amount of
serious consideration that went into designing them from the point of view
of satisfying the specific criteria for socialist institutions was actually less
than might at first be thought.

In terms of the structures that were eventually formed, state farms
(*sovkhoz*), which were the property of the government and in which the
manager conformed to ministerial directives, were distinguished from collective farms (*kolkhoz*), which were supposed to be self-governing cooperatives
constituted voluntarily. The actual resistance of peasants to collectivisation
led to the *artel* being accepted at least initially as the prevalent type of collective, although this formation did not at all resemble the pre-war *artel* in its
most important aspects.[27] Three major types of collective farms came into
existence in 1930 – the commune, the *artel* and the association – which were
distinguished by the extent to which the means of production were socialised.
No exact definition was adopted, but in general in the commune everything
was supposed to be socialised, in the *artel* some branches of agriculture could
remain in private hands, and in associations animals and implements were
held individually.[28] A general meeting of the collective farm was supposed to
elect a board of control, and work brigades of a number of household units
were usually the standard internal subdivision within them.

Disputes sometimes flared up among the party leadership over the
precise ideological significance of collective farms. Some saw them as only
transitional types of economy, since some private elements remained,
whereas others saw them as actual examples of socialist economy in agriculture. The progression from association to *artel* to commune was usually
seen as a movement from a lower to a higher form of farming. Again the
distinction between the modernisation of agriculture and its transformation
into socialist forms of management was often blurred in such debates.

If in agriculture the collective farm was seen as a key socialist institution, then what about in the industrial sector of the Soviet economy?
Various apparently socialistic forms of industrial economy were fostered in

the USSR in the 1930s. For example a movement to create 'production collectives' in industry came into being very early in 1930. In these collectives the work accomplished by all members was recorded as a whole, rather than the work done by each person being measured individually. Wages were then divided equally among members from overall income, instead of being distributed on an individual basis.[29] Marx's principle 'from each according to their ability, to each according to their needs', was on the face of it being partially implemented, as each member of the production collective was contributing what labour power they could manage. However, such forms might be seen by some as islets of equality within an overall framework of inequality. Unless the overall framework of economy had been correctly established, then resentment about inequality was unlikely to be overcome by such relatively minor socialistic sub-structures.

## The view from afar

Various Russian émigré economists watched developments in the Soviet economy with a mixture of fear, awe and relief. Fear of a great success, awe at a possible new dawn, and eventual relief that it appeared in some measure at least a failure. However, some émigrés provided insightful and relatively objective commentary on the structure of Stalinist economy. For example S.N. Prokopovich highlighted a peculiar feature of what he termed 'planned-out economic organisation' – the national economy had been merged into a single, very large governmental organisation, with the result that people in it had ceased to have any personal interest in economy. He astutely realised that in fact there had been various different ways of organising the centralised management of industry. Instead of a single plan of production based solely on technical considerations elaborated from the centre, each individual industrial unit or trust could have worked out a production and distribution plan taking into account production costs, fuel, labour, amortisation, transport and so on. It could then have set sale prices making allowances for available purchasing power and the need for profit, that is using calculations made through economic values rather than simply technical ones.[30] Overall coordination could have been achieved through market-style adjustments undertaken over time.

In other areas of his diagnosis Prokopovich was less insightful. He provocatively characterised Stalinist economy as the negation of all economic principles, or as what could be called anti-economy. The three principles that lay at the basis of Stalinist nationalised industry were said to be:

1  the annihilation of a quantitative relation between labour productivity and wages;
2  the abolition of the unity of industrial management through economic calculation;
3  the use of a single purely material economic plan.[31]

Prokopovich erroneously predicted only industrial degradation and decay as the result of the further application of these principles in the USSR, and perhaps he was proved wrong in the prediction because his outlined principles were not fully accurate.

It wasn't only economists who focused their attention on the USSR from overseas. The pragmatist philosopher John Dewey visited the USSR and published his *Impressions of Soviet Russia* in 1928. Dewey quickly realised that, in order to be a success, communist economy required changes outside of the purely economic realm. He wrote that the problem was not only replacing capitalistic by collectivistic economic institutions, but also of substituting a collective mentality for the individualistic psychology inherited from the previous epoch.[32] This led to the extraordinary importance of education and propaganda, which were very often confounded and even identified as unity. Regarding the purely economic realm of the Soviet system, Dewey explained that there was an element of the situation in the USSR that he thought was psychologically unique:

> there is the state Industrial Plan which covers or attempts to cover a general plan for the development of industry for periods of five years ahead. Those plans are made of course, by economists and technologists, engineers and industrialists working together; but the interesting part of the situation is that managers of factories and laborers in factories are taken into some intellectual partnership. They know what the plans and purposes and the system of the Central Planning Committee of the State are; and they get a sense of being partners and fellow-workers in the development of these large plans.[33]

This was not of course completely accurate, as factory workers were not often 'taken into partnership' with respect of designing plans, and nor were industrialists (in the capitalist sense) involved in working together with other planning personnel, as they had been expropriated from their positions of power soon after 1917. However as an account of how one type of planning might have operated, Dewey's approach is worth considering.

## Corporate economy in the 1930s

Developments in the American economy in the 1930s were always not totally antithetical to those occurring in Stalin's Russia. As noted previously, the US economists Berle and Means saw the divorce of ownership of the means of production from control that had occurred in the US economy by the 1930s to constitute a new form of organisation of the capitalist system. They called this new form 'collective capitalism', in which stock and security ownership became the dominant form of wealth control. The crucial feature was seen to be that those who owned all the wealth no longer managed it and those who managed it no longer owned it, this change having significant consequences for how the market-control system operated.[34] In the USSR by the 1930s a somewhat similar but by no means an exactly parallel development had occurred. Those who owned all the wealth (nominally 'the people') did not control it, rather control was vested in a small group of elite party personnel, bureaucrats and planners, somewhat akin to the managers in 'collective capitalism', whilst those who controlled it (party planners) did not own it, at least in strictly legal terms.

In terms of system justification, whilst production priorities in 1930s capitalism were said to flow from consideration of genuine consumer requirements, in 1930s Soviet socialism the highest echelons of planners set production priorities allegedly based on long-term strategic considerations relating to the good of the nation as a whole. Of course in reality in 1930s Western capitalism, consumer desires were constantly manipulated through advertising and the propagation of status emulation fashions, whilst in 1930s Soviet socialism the strategic goals were subject to constant contestation and alteration by sectoral interest groups and those planners who were currently in Stalin's favour. This does not mean that the Soviet and US economies in the 1930s were by nature the same, but it does suggest that some of the underlying forces generating economic activity in both systems were not totally dissimilar.

## Leon Trotsky on Stalinist economy

From his impotent position of exile, Trotsky's attitude to the Soviet economy in the 1930s was fundamentally ambiguous. While he praised the policies of collectivisation and rapid planned industrialisation, which he interpreted as being in some respects a direct copy of the Left Oppositions' platform, he was critical of over-optimistic plan targets and rigid orders from above, which were characterised as adventuristic. Trotsky also highlighted the low quality of much Soviet industrial production, with quantity of goods being valued far above quality, and the declining conditions of workers.[35] The quality issue had knock-on consequences in that the need for repairs escalated and half-finished projects abounded. However a sceptic might want to characterise Trotsky's criticisms as sour grapes, as he did not simultaneously provide a detailed alternative programme for Soviet development based on genuinely socialist principles. When in power in the early 1920s Trotsky had been as comparably ruthless as Stalin was in similar circumstances, and had supported the further extension of comparable planning methods.

In respect of characterising the Soviet system generally, Trotsky believed that the USSR had become a bureaucratically deformed workers state. This meant that whilst state ownership of property and economic planning still existed, the party bureaucracy had usurped power away from the workers.

Whether this bureaucracy constituted a new ruling class or was simply some type of social caste was a much-debated question. Two possibilities for the future of the USSR were said to exist, either capitalist restoration or genuine workers power; from Trotsky's viewpoint the former eventually occurred under Yeltsin. However, Trotsky never specified in detail how planning would function under genuine workers' power, perhaps suggesting that it was easier to be a critic of planning than an inventor.

## The Keynesian challenge

The development of central planning in the USSR in the 1930s coincided with the onset of the great depression in the West, which began with the Wall Street crash in 1929. The Cambridge economist J.M. Keynes provided one of the key responses to this development in terms of mainstream economic theory. In his *Treatise on Money* of 1930 Keynes proposed to find a method to describe the dynamic laws governing the passage of the monetary system from one position of equilibrium to another, this obviously being of major relevance to understanding how the disequilibrium position of the great depression could be prevented from reoccurring. That Keynes was also concerned with the challenge from Soviet central planning in this work is apparent from his statement that, if there was recurrent deflation, then 'our present regime of capitalistic individualism will assuredly be replaced by a far-reaching socialism'.[36] His economic work was of course designed specifically to avert this particular societal replacement from happening.

By the time of the publication of the *General Theory of Employment, Interest and Money* in 1936 Keynes was even more concerned about the future of capitalistic individualism. In this work he wrote:

> no obvious case is made out for a system of State Socialism ... It is not the ownership of the instruments of production which it is important for the State to assume. If the State is able to determine the aggregate amount of resources devoted to augmenting the instruments and the basic rate of reward to those who own them, it will have accomplished all that is necessary.[37]

Keynes still believed in 1936 that the existing system (by which he meant British capitalism in the 1930s) did not seriously misemploy factors of production, despite his acknowledgement of the suffering caused by mass unemployment. His concern with the ownership of the instruments of production was revealing, since in the USSR these instruments had been socialised and were the focus of plan directives. By regulating both the extent and the rewards of investment within capitalism Keynes hoped that socialised control could be limited to only these particular elements of the system.

Keynes had visited Soviet Russia in 1925 and presented a paper entitled 'The Economic Transition in England' to an audience in Moscow on 15 September. Employing Commons' conception of three economic orders through which the world was progressing – epochs characterised by scarcity, abundance and stabilisation – Keynes explained:

> Some of you in Russia will not agree with me in seeking help in these matters from a reformed and remodelled Liberalism, which above all things, shall not, if my idea is realised, be a class party. Leninism – so it seems to me – is at the same time a persecuting religion and an experimental technique. Capitalism too is at the same time a religion, which is much more tolerant, however, than Leninism is.[38]

Sometime later, in December 1931, Keynes published 'A Survey of the Present Position of Socialism'. Here he analysed socialism as being essentially schizoid, as having two heads and two hearts that were always at war with each other. The first was concerned to act in a way that was 'economically sound', the second wanted to act in a way which was 'economically unsound'.[39] Keynes himself defined the socialist proposition thus, to obtain political power with a view to doing what was economically sound in order that the community may become rich enough to afford what was economically unsound.[40] By framing the question in this manner Keynes implied that he was on the face of it unsure that the socialist experiment would be successful. At a deeper level it suggested that Keynes saw socialistic intervention as a way of bettering the performance of the existing economy, not of radically transforming structures and mechanisms to conform to a new view of what the economy should be. Keynes admitted never to fully understanding Marx's vision, and in this admission he was perhaps correct.

## A partial balance sheet for and against planning

In traditional socialist theory at least, imperative planning could have many virtues as against market-control systems of economy. A fully symmetrical coordination of branches of the economy, an accurate correlation of production and distribution, and the elimination of waste and unnecessary duplication might be seen as a few such virtues. These type of benefits flow from the rationalistic ability to fully harmonise all the elements of an economy in relation to all others, something that (according to socialist doctrine at least) would occur only accidentally in capitalist systems of economy.

Tugan-Baranovsky's pioneering work on trade cycle theory had highlighted disproportionality as a key factor causing the ebb and flow of economic life in the UK in the nineteenth century, something that planning had been touted as being able to overcome. That the rationalist dream appeared to fail in the Russian context had been suggested by some to be because the amount, accuracy and speed of knowledge required to be comprehended by planning organs was beyond the abilities of those involved. Others have indicated that some changes in the specific nature of planning that might have improved its capabilities were at variance with the need of the political dictatorship to control the operation of economics units.[41]

It could be argued that many of the difficulties encountered by the Soviet economic system in the 1930s were the natural result of an effort to transform a backward country into a great industrial power in a very short period of time, rather than being a consequence of a system of economic planning in itself. While this might be a not unreasonable argument, it glosses over the fact that creating a socialist economy in terms of institutions and structures was often relegated to second place as against industrialisation *per se* in the USSR in the 1930s. Those who had originated the Marxian variant of socialism had in no way seen industrialisation as a key requirement of planning policy, since it was to be advanced capitalist countries that would first make the change to socialist forms of economy.

In a philosophical sense the entire history of the USSR could thus be interpreted as a giant category mistake, in which the facts of Soviet history were represented as belonging to one logical type of category ('planning'), when actually they really belonged to another very different type ('industrialisation'). The failure to clearly distinguish between these two separate goals permeated much of the early history of Soviet planning, and had an important legacy for Third World states, in that they often assumed that Soviet planning was a system designed primarily for industrialisation. In truth planned economy had been first conceived as a system to follow on from advanced capitalism in its post-industrial phase, and indeed could only be a success in the conditions of relative abundance that post-industrial societies could generate.

In terms of concrete results, the Soviet economy had certainly become much more self-sufficient by the end of the 1930s. For example the Soviet share in world trade fell from 2.5 per cent in 1931 to 1.3 per cent in 1936.[42] Whether this was a positive or negative development depends upon the perspective adopted. As evaluated by Boris Brutzkus, during the first five-year plan very large levels of capital investment were achieved in a poverty-stricken country, and a very backward nation was compelled to make great savings that would have been unlikely to occur in capitalism. In particular in heavy industry Brutzkus called the production successes remarkable, but then contrasted this with the shockingly inadequate living conditions of the workers who serviced this industry. Indeed for Brutzkus the essence of what he referred to as Soviet Russian planned economy was an inner union between economics and politics, the economic system having being conceived entirely from a political point of view.[43] From this perspective Stalinist economy was the supreme expression of the primacy

of the political, not the negation of politics that Marx had initially predicted as the outcome of socialist control.

## What was the Soviet economy?

Both from a neoclassical and a Marxist position the USSR in the 1930s
had some type of centrally planned economy that could be contrasted dia-
metrically with its absolute opposite, the free market economy of the USA.
Various terms have been suggested to characterise the Soviet economy
within these frameworks, terms such as imperative planning, administrative-
command system, bureaucratic collectivism, socialist economy and non-
monetary economy. All of these categorisations have some degree of
appropriateness but abstract from only some of the features present in the
system, either the mechanism of plan construction, the system of bureaucratic control and property ownership, the hierarchy of influence of monetary purchasing power against party diktat and so on.

For example for Alec Nove, the centralised planning system imposed
under Stalin was a *sui generis* war economy, similar to a capitalist war
economy, with central control over resource allocation, politically imposed
priorities, price control and rationing. In another view Soviet planning was
not actually economic planning at all, but rather a means of intimidating
the labour force into continual acquiescence. Overfulfillment of goals was
always heavily praised, whereas underfulfillment was harshly criticised, yet
both were deviations from the plan that led to distortions in economic
performance, that should have been seen as equally detrimental in a true
planning system.

However from the point of view of institutionalism both the USSR and
the USA in the 1930s had mixed economic systems, with elements of
social, bureaucratic and private control intertwined, although the balance
of the mix differed significantly in the two economies. The party-
administered central planning institutions of the Soviet economy can then
(from this viewpoint) be contrasted with the manager-administered market
control institutions of the US economy, and the place of the individual firm
in the Soviet planning system contrasted with the place of the single enterprise in the US market-control system. Industrial units in both systems
attempted to satisfy consumer desires by manufacturing products that
were apparently required of them, which were determined either by plan
control mechanisms or market survey estimations of future demand, and
small groups of power-network-connected elites controlled the political
priorities and national budgets administered by the state.

In the Soviet economy in the 1930s sectoral interests played an important role in determining plan priorities. For example the steel industry and
the coal industry formed powerful lobbying groups that attempted to exert
pressure on planning bodies through individual commissariat representation. A not totally dissimilar phenomenon could be seen in the US

economy, where large and powerful business corporations attempted to influence government policy decisions through lobbying and informal networks of influence. Anti-trust policies began in the USA with the Sherman Act in 1890, but some firms still continued to attempt to fix prices after this date, whilst the idea of monopolistic or imperfect competition in Western economics received much attention in the 1930s and beyond. This suggested that the prevalence of perfect competition as outlined in neoclassical economics was quite limited, and hence justifying the existence of market-control systems on this basis was a misnomer.

What then was the crucial distinction between the US and the Soviet economy? It could be argued that the most crucial difference related not to any purely economic structure or priority, but rather simply to the fact that the USSR dared to oppose the USA both ideologically and geopolitically. In confronting nascent US hegemony the USSR had set itself up as a working alternative to market-control systems, at least nominally in ideology if less so in the practical reality of its economy. From this perspective, if the Soviet economy was composed of structures and mechanisms that were not always that dissimilar to those that existed in the USA – after all, things usually only change so that they can stay the same – then its real radical nature consisted mainly in having the galling and effrontery insolence to imply simply through its existence that there might be another way of structuring economic life.

# 6 Conclusions for future economy

## The Soviet economy in 1940

What had the Bolshevik effort actually achieved by the time of the start of the Second World War and the (at least temporary) congealing of the particular system of planning that was the legacy of October 1917? On the positive side it had shown that revolutionary socialists could maintain political control in a given country for a significant period of time and institute various fundamental economic changes. Investment in heavy industry had been increased on a massive scale and agricultural production had been radically transformed. On the negative side it had shown that, in the Russian context at least, the price to be paid for this Bolshevik control was very high indeed, both in human and material costs. Working conditions in much of industry remained gruellingly harsh and the peasantry had been forced against their will into large-scale collectivisation. In terms of liberating the species-being of all humanity – Marx's underlying goal – little had been achieved, as most people still toiled in very difficult working conditions for long hours with little capacity for leisure amidst authoritarian social structures. It is true that universal education for example was receiving much more attention than in Tsarist times, even despite Kokovtsov's pre-war efforts, but this education had become merged with propaganda to a very frightening degree.

Moreover the particular forms of socialist economy created by the Bolsheviks were hugely problematic, both in structure and in results, with inflexible vertical relationships between party, planners and 'the people' becoming quickly set in stone. On the eve of the Second World War the Soviet economy was in a position strong enough to successfully fight against Nazi aggression, but the human and ecological sacrifices that had been made to get to this position were monumental. Whether such sacrifices were a necessity no matter what system of economy was in operation is a very controversial question, but it is difficult to see how elements such as violent purges on a mass scale assisted preparations for the forthcoming battle against Hitler, except perhaps by installing a sweat-inducing fear of disobeying orders, a Fascistic method in itself.

When Germany invaded Poland in September 1939, the all-American boy wonder George Orson Welles was contemplating the making of his first feature film for the moviemaking branch of the Radio-Keith-Orpheum Corporation. Circumstances conspired to change this from an adaptation of Joseph Conrad's *The Heart of Darkness* to developing Herman J. Mankiewicz's idea for *American*. Of course, *Citizen Kane* is now regarded as the best film ever made and a biting critique of the loneliness sometimes engendered by the great concentrations of personal wealth that are a by-product of capitalist forms of economy. Association with moneyed splendour fatally polluted Charles Foster Kane's personal relationships, and the emptiness of Xanadu (and later the resplendent decay of the magnificent Ambersons) would serve as a potent allegory for the heavy price paid by some for the American dream. William Randolf Hearst was not best pleased with Welles' impudent efforts, and the boy wonder never fully recovered his youthful zest of genius thereafter.

And yet a cinematic edition of 'News on the March' might well have reported on a sparkling new invention from way out East, the five-year plan, which promised a bright new dawn without any such materialistically imprisoned loneliness, with restructured social and property relations to boot. Some cynics might detect a touch of evil in such false promises, but it is the task of the objective scholar to dissect meticulously the new Soviet economy for anything genuine, anything that really was egalitarian and truly rational. Were there any such things, or has the meaning of the Russian Rosebud been lost forever?

## Is a rationalist transformation of society possible?

The answer to this frosty question depends, as always, on the perspective adopted. From a neoclassical perspective, markets are natural mechanisms that operate efficiently only without external interference. Hence, any rationalist attempt to replace them by planning would necessarily fail, just as any attempt to tamper with the law of gravity would fail. From a traditional socialist perspective irrational market processes still require replacement by rational planning, and perhaps the USSR failed due to a number of contextual factors such as overseas hostility, the backwardness of Russia itself, the creation of a parasitic party bureaucracy and a fatal loss of nerve by Mikhail Gorbachev. From an institutionalist perspective both markets and planning bodies are institutions that operate within complex and multi-layered economic systems. Transforming these systems rationally is possible but fraught with pitfalls, as the concomitant transformation of habitual human behaviour is also required.

Elements of all the above conceptions can be seen to have some degree of relevance to understanding the revolutionary Russian economy, although each individual person must specify the particular mix of thought to apply, and also add any further elements that might be thought currently lacking.

Moreover, through this book readers should begin to understand that having different views of how the market economy functions would dramatically affect the type of planning system chosen to replace it. If there was a belief that markets worked according to classical theory, then the planning mechanisms designed to replace them might be one thing; if there was a belief that markets functioned in a neoclassical manner, then the planning institutions designed to replace them might be a whole other ball-game. And if markets are part of a highly complex system of networks and structures which function in different ways at different times under different legal systems and through various patterns of human behaviour – ideological, sexual, familial – and under the influence of particular conjunctural phenomena and myriad political atmospheres, then designing a system for replacing them becomes a far from simple operation. That the Bolsheviks ultimately failed in the circumstances of 'backward' Tsarist Russia is perhaps then a little more understandable, if not totally forgivable.

The psychologist Wilhelm Reich provided a particularly original analysis of the reasons for the failure of Soviet economy. He argued that the socialisation of production by itself could not effect a change in the conditions of economic slavery found in capitalist economy, since to regard purely economic processes as the essence of human bio-social life was woefully mistaken.[1] The authoritarian personality engendered by capitalist and also by Stalinist economy was the result of malformed human sexual character structure, including repressed sexual desires, and a concomitant failure to abolish restrictive social structures such as the family. Put simply, an authoritarian inter-sexual order survived in Russia after 1917, an order that affected fundamentally the structures chosen to regulate economic life. Whilst this mono-causal association of Soviet failure with an authoritarian character structure might be overly simplistic, Reich's attempt to reach beyond economic concerns (narrowly conceived) was refreshing and could be seen as one important piece of a multifaceted jigsaw of explanation.

## Is a rationalist transformation of society desirable?

From an Edmund Burke-inspired conservative perspective, all rationalistic attempts to meddle in the organic progress of human affairs inevitably ended in failure, due to the inability of rationalists to understanding that social processes occurred (at least in part) at a sub-rational and non-conscious level of instinct, desire and emotion. Rationalistic social engineering had failed in the past because it was beyond the reach of the conscious human mind to fully comprehend its own actions in such realms of activity, and intervention without complete comprehension led to unpredictable and sometimes disastrous consequences. Moreover, the equality that socialists pined for was impossible to achieve in practice, since differences between individual people were innate and were impossible to overcome by means of government policy. Thus from this perspective the actually real is forever rational and the yet-to-be-real is forever irrational.

These are certainly an elegant set of arguments, but are they at all accurate? Conveniently, one element was beyond final a priori refutation, since the conservative did not have to specify exactly what was lacking in the argument of the rationalist, since it was by nature beyond human comprehension. Even if there was some truth in the conservative position, it might be partially accommodated from within the perspective of the rationalist if scope was deliberately allowed for continued input from the sub-rational and non-conscious levels. Past failures occurred by denying the existence of such levels of social reality; consequently by accepting and including the sub-rational and non-conscious levels in the decision-making process, the rationalist might in theory accommodate the conservative position. As to overcoming inequality, it was equality of opportunity that was desired by socialists, not equality of outcome. But would a sophisticated rationalist at the beginning of the twenty first century still want to create an economy that is comprehensively 'planned' in order to achieve their egalitarian aims?

## What is a planned economy?

J.K. Galbraith has usefully distinguished between two senses of the phrase 'economic planning'. As undertaken by an industrial firm, planning consisted in foreseeing the actions required between the initiation and completion of the production of commodities. For example in one restrictive definition given in the USA in 1929, production planning was 'the systematic preparation of manufacturing data, so arranged as to facilitate accurate determination of delivery dates'.[2] However, as viewed by an orthodox economist it was something much more fundamental, consisting of replacing free markets and prices with an authoritarian determination of what will be produced through an all-encompassing planning document.[3] The two senses were not mutually exclusive, but whilst the first was seen by many as a natural part of market-control systems they viewed the second as an alien invention.

The absurdity of this polarised view is apparent if it is considered how much planning (albeit of a particular type) occurs within firms, within markets and within governments in relation to economic affairs in Western-style market economies. All firms, markets and governments produce documents which purport to set targets for the future in relation to specific areas of activity, documents which are sometimes even called 'plans'. On an extrapolation of this more nuanced view, market-control systems can be seen themselves as one particular variety of planned economy, the Soviet economy in the 1930s being another quite different variety of planned economy. There might be an infinite number of possible planned economies, it just all depends on exactly what you mean by 'planning'. Examined from this perspective, creating a socialistic planned economy means simply giving a rational basis to the planning which is actually desired to exist by many, but might not yet be possible in market-control forms of planning due to the unequal distribution of various elements in systems such as property rights.

F.A. Hayek's work on the use of knowledge in an economy is worth considering at this point, Hayek being famed as an economist in the Austrian tradition who argued that conscious planning that mimicked the market would be impossible to accomplish successfully because of the decentralised distribution of knowledge throughout society. In fact Hayek agreed that all economic activity was in one sense planning, involving a complex set of interrelated decisions about the allocation of available resources, but he highlighted the way in which the knowledge on which plans were based was communicated. In a market system decentralised planning by many separate people occurred spontaneously, whereas in a Soviet-type economy, planning meant central control of the whole economy through one unified plan.[4] Hence for Hayek market-control systems employed planning mechanisms that operated successfully, whereas Soviet-style economies used planning mechanisms that failed to deliver positive results.

From a historical perspective, this conception of the market as actually being planning was not even known to those Bolsheviks who began the task of creating a socialist economy after 1917. Could or should decentralised planning of the Hayek type be replicated in a rationalistic transformation of economy? Given the speed of development of new forms of communication such as the internet, some might argue that it could be, although others would undoubtedly argue the opposite. It might be asked whether planning that attempts to out-market the market really has any underlying rationale, although the idea of market failure might provide one particular example of such a reason.

## Some notable continuities and discontinuities around 1917

In the true meaning of the word, a 'revolution' means a (360 degree) return to the point of origin, rather than a (180 degree) fundamental change in direction. The Bolshevik revolution encompassed both of these meanings to various degrees. What were some of the most readily apparent economic continuities before and after 1917?

A very significant continuity through 1917 was the crucial role of the state in fostering economic development. With both Witte before 1917 and Stalin in the 1930s, the Russian and Soviet government was a prime mover in business affairs, although the precise definition of its role did change dramatically. If the state only assisted and set individual policies to encourage private initiative before 1917, then after 1917 the state's role mushroomed dramatically to creating the overall framework and also to setting the detailed goals of all economic activity. Bukharin theorised the growing role of the government before 1917 as state capitalism, and Lenin continued this type of approach after 1917. However exactly when state capitalism became state socialism was a very contentious question, one that was open to many different interpretations.

In terms of industrial structure, in the period after 1900 the Tsarist economy had seen the formation of many industrial syndicates, for example a large metallurgical syndicate was created with an agreement to regulate and divide production, prices and market share. Syndicates for mined ore, iron pipes, farm machinery and railcars were also formed at this time. Bukharin had theorised these developments in 1915 as the organisational forms of international capitalist economy. However, this process was repeated after 1917 in the Bolshevik economy, when in March 1922 the formation of a number of industrial syndicates occurred to monopolise the sales system in order to prevent possible falls in prices. At the end of 1922 eighteen syndicates had been created in the textile, mining, tobacco, agricultural machinery and various other sectors. This suggests that syndicate combination was a response common to both capitalist and (transitional) socialist economic structures.

In terms of identifying discontinuities, ideologically at least 1917 marked a genuine and fundamental break with the past, signalling an abrupt and decisive change from religious and monarchistic aristocracy to atheistic and egalitarian Communist Party control. However, looking beyond the treacherous veil of ideology, in both periods a tiny self-appointed elite determined the political and economic structures governing the reality of the lives of millions of ordinary peasants and workers across Russia. Both ideological systems claimed to have the best interests of all at heart, although these 'best interests' were defined very differently in each system, and in both systems those at the top of the pile lived very privileged lives compared to those near the bottom. By 1940 the market-control system of planning that functioned in the Tsarist period had been comprehensively replaced by a very different state-controlled system of planning, although it could reasonably be argued that no significant increase in the level of genuinely democratic participation in economic management had actually occurred after 1917.

Some notable improvements in living conditions undoubtedly occurred through 1917, although some aggravation of previously existing conditions took place also. As social reality is infinitely complex, no final ledger book of account can be provided for Soviet history, saying definitively whether Bolshevik control was a positive or negative development overall. For some people it was certainly positive, for others it was a very negative experience. But the crucial feature that this book has hopefully provided is help in understanding how having different perspectives on economic structures and mechanisms leads to different conclusions as to outcome. How to finally decide between competing perspectives is not something that is answered here.

## The end of the beginning?

The Russian and Soviet experience in creating new types of economy was certainly dramatic, for a time influential and initially at least quite radical, but it was also very often cruel, usually unforgiving and sometimes wholly negative. At the beginning some saw it as a beacon of hope in an era of bloody mechanised war, but many see it today as a failed and discredited experiment that cost millions of lives from all over the world, one that has cast the general idea of socialism in a very bad light indeed. After the Second World War the USA always justified its overseas intervention against recently installed socialist governments by implied reference to the evils of Stalinism, and it must be acknowledged by all concerned that they really did have a valid point.

However, history is never anything other than dialectical, and from the ashes of the Soviet experience, lessons could be drawn today by those with the insight to see them. One of the most important might be that any future attempt at a rationalist transformation of society should have a fully elaborated conception of exactly how the new society will operate, otherwise the vacuum will be occupied by shallow opportunists who employ cunning social manipulation for personal aggrandisement.[5] A fully elaborated conception means one hundred detailed volumes on each of a hundred different parts of the socialist system worked out by hundreds of honourable scholars over decades. And a dozen alternatives of the same as back up. And a dozen versions of how this system might evolve over time.[6] And then be prepared to discard all of this if the circumstances of the day required it.

Another important lesson might be that socialists today should pay less attention to questions related to fostering industrial development, and more to solving the problems of egalitarian industrial structure. It was the capitalist *system* of economy that was criticised in classical Marxism, not the purely economic results that it generated. The fetishism of plan targets witnessed in the USSR in the 1930s could be interpreted as a twisted echo of performance indicators found in capitalist economy. Consequently it might nowadays be thought wise to forgo some of the material outputs achieved by post-industrial capital, in order to facilitate a more just and equitable system of relations between and within the constituent structures of new and more progressive forms of economy.

Thus a real question for socialists today is not so much how to achieve power, but what to do successfully with it afterwards. It appears obvious from the perspective of today that mass slaughter and sadistic mendacity were not good marketing jingles for Soviet socialists to initially adopt. Readers might now begin to question the socialist credentials of all-powerful dictators like Stalin, viewing 'socialist' and 'dictator' as mutually exclusive terms. If it was believed that the circumstances necessitated a dictator, then it could be concluded that the time was not ripe for genuine socialism.

Still another lesson might be that the exploitation that socialism was created to overcome really lies at a much more fundamental level that the extraction of surplus value from the working class by those owning the means of production. Exploitative social relations could be a function of the unequal distribution of power throughout society; all types of power, be it financial, economic, political, sexual, technical, bureaucratic, physical, emotional, psychological, intellectual and many other types. From this perspective, only when all types of power are distributed equally among all persons of the globe, will a truly non-exploitative society finally be possible. Attempting to create a socialist society that still harboured an unequal distribution of power might inevitably result in 'socialist exploitation', a great irony but a negative reality no different at all from 'capitalist exploitation'.

On the other hand, perhaps people could learn to resist the opportunity to use the unequal distribution of power for personal gain, and thus a socialist society could function with skewed power relations. It is for the reader to finally decide on this issue, as on all others, the author only hopes that the reader appreciates the process of decision-making. After all, in socialism pleasure (both mental and physical) and personal happiness should be the final goal of all activity – or should it? Thinking about it, after being released from the burden of continuous monotonous work under capitalism, what would people do all the time? I leave it to the readers' imagination to provide the answer, but hunter, fisherman, shepherd and critic might be a good starting-point, to which might be added physicist, actor, art connoisseur, gymnast, gravedigger, toilet attendant and mortician. Just not all on the same afternoon.

# Notes

## 1 Introduction to Russian economy

1 Colin Clark, *A Critique of Russian Statistics* (London: Macmillan, 1939), title page.
2 'Intermediate-level' in this context means intermediate between a purely research-based monograph and a postgraduate level textbook, but also intermediate between the subjects of history and economics themselves.
3 R.A. Solo, *Economic Organizations and Social Systems* (Ann Arbor: University of Michigan, 2000), p. ix.
4 Ludwig Wittgenstein, *Tractatus Logico-Philosophicus* (London: RKP, 1981), p. 31.
5 David Lewis, *On the Plurality of Worlds* (Oxford: Blackwell, 1986), pp. 2–4.
6 E.H. Carr, *What is History?* (Harmondsworth: Penguin, 1961), p. 103.
7 Ibid., p. 97.
8 This account is taken from Arcadius Kahan, *The Plow, the Hammer and the Knout* (Chicago: Chicago University, 1985).
9 R.W. Davies, *Soviet Economic Development from Lenin to Khrushchev* (Cambridge: Cambridge University Press, 1998), p. 6.
10 M.C. Howard and J.E. King, *A History of Marxian Economics* (Princeton: Princeton University Press, 1989), vol. 1, p. 130.
11 Peter Gatrell, *The Tsarist Economy, 1850–1917* (London: Batsford, 1986), p. 100.
12 W.E. Mosse, *An Economic History of Russia* (London: Tauris, 1996), p. 5.
13 W.W. Rostow, *Theorists of Economic Growth from David Hume to the Present* (Oxford: Oxford University Press, 1990), p. 5.
14 Arcadius Kahan, *Russian Economic History* (Chicago: Chicago University Press, 1989), p. 2; M.E. Falkus, *The Industrialisation of Russia* (London: Macmillan, 1972), p. 17.
15 R.M. Sundrum, *Economic Growth in Theory and Practice* (London: Macmillan, 1990), pp. 54–61.
16 Walter Eltis, 'Harrod-Domar Growth', *The New Palgrave Dictionary of Economics* (London: Macmillan, 1987), vol. 2, p. 602.
17 Gatrell, *The Tsarist Economy*, p. 202.
18 W.W. Rostow, *The Stages of Economic Growth* (Cambridge: Cambridge University Press, 1971), pp. 4–11.
19 Alexander Gerschenkron, *Europe in the Russian Mirror* (Cambridge: Cambridge University Press, 1970), pp. 99–102.
20 D.C. North, *Structure and Change in Economic History* (New York: Norton, 1981), p. 171.
21 D.R. Fusfeld, 'The Development of Economic Institutions', *Journal of Economic Issues*, December 1977, pp. 752–4.

22 P.I. Lyashchenko, *History of the National Economy of Russia to the 1917 Revolution* (New York: Macmillan, 1949), pp. 422–3.
23 Janos Kornai, *Anti-Equilibrium* (Amsterdam: North-Holland, 1971).
24 Janos Kornai, *Vision and Reality, Market and State* (New York: Harvester, 1990), p. 2.
25 P.J.D. Wiles, *Communist International Economics* (Oxford: Blackwell, 1968), pp. 30–3.
26 V.I. Lenin, *Materialism and Empirio-Criticism* (Moscow: Progress, 1947), p. 303.
27 E.M. Kayden and A.N. Antsiferov, *The Cooperative Movement in Russia During the War* (New Haven: Yale University Press, 1929), p. 4.
28 Kahan, *Russian Economic History*, p. 6.
29 PRO, FO 881/5674, p. 6 and p. 11.
30 Frederick Engels, 'Anti-During', in Alec Nove and I.D. Thatcher (eds) *Markets and Socialism* (Aldershot: Elgar, 1994), pp. 23–4.

## 2 Tsarist economy

1 Ernesto Screpanti and Stefano Zamagni, *An Outline of the History of Economic Thought* (Oxford: Clarendon, 1993), p. 176.
2 Joseph Schumpeter, *Business Cycles* (New York: McGraw-Hill, 1939), vol. 1, p. 305.
3 J.M. Keynes, *Treatise on Probability* (London: Macmillan, 1921), p. 386.
4 James D. White, *Lenin* (London: Palgrave, 2001), p. 41.
5 V.I. Lenin, *Collected Works* vol. 3 (London: L&W, 1960), pp. 67–9.
6 Peter Waldron, *The End of Imperial Russia* (London: Macmillan, 1997), pp. 2–4; J.D. White, *The Russian Revolution, 1917–21* (London: Elgar, 1994) pp. 16–17.
7 PRO, FO 881/5674, p. 16.
8 Waldron, *The End of Imperial Russia*, p. 33.
9 Joseph Schumpeter, *Imperialism and Social Classes* (Oxford: Blackwell, 1951), p. 81.
10 V.K. Dmitriev, *Economic Essays on Value, Competition and Utility* (Cambridge: Cambridge University Press, 1974), pp. 147–8.
11 P.I. Lyashchenko, *History of the National Economy of Russia to the 1917 Revolution* (New York: Macmillan, 1949), pp. 675–6.
12 M.E. Falkus, *The Industrialisation of Russia* (London: Macmillan, 1972), pp. 62–3.
13 Waldron, *The End of Imperial Russia*, p. 64.
14 Arcadius Kahan, *Russian Economic History* (Chicago: Chicago University Press, 1989), p. 103.
15 Figures calculated from Kahan, *Russian Economic History*, p. 62, Table 1.31.
16 Gregory Sokolnikov, *Soviet Policy in Public Finance* (Stanford: Stanford University, 1931), pp. 8–9.
17 P.V. Ol', *Foreign Capital in Russia* (New York: Garland, 1983), p. xiv.
18 S.A. Pervushin, *Khozyaistvennaya kon'yunktura* (Moscow: Ekonomicheskaya Zhizn, 1925), pp. 162–5.
19 Ibid., p. 191.
20 Dmitriev, *Economic Essays on Value, Competition and Utility*, p. 172.
21 Sokolnikov, *Soviet Policy in Public Finance*, pp. 442–3.
22 T. Emmons and W. Vucinich (eds), *The Zemstvo in Russia* (Cambridge: Cambridge University Press, 1982), pp. 5–23.

23 Waldron, *The End of Imperial Russia*, p. 53.
24 A.I. Chuprov, *Po povodu ukaza 9 Noyabrya 1906* (Moscow: Sabashnikov, 1908), p. 41.
25 Ibid., p. 9.
26 Yanni Kotsonis, *Making Peasants Backward* (London: Macmillan, 1999), pp. 53–4.
27 Peter Gatrell, *Government, Industry and Rearmament in Russia* (Cambridge: Cambridge University Press, 1994), p. 92.
28 V.N. Kokovstov, *Out of My Past: Memoirs of Count Kokovtsov* (Stanford: Stanford University, 1935), pp. 457–9.
29 'Otchet Kokovtsov komitetu finansov', *Krasnyi Arkhiv*, vol. 3, 1925, p. 29.
30 Olga Crisp, *Studies in the Russian Economy Before 1914* (London: Macmillan, 1976), p. 206.
31 'K peregovoram Kokovtsova o zaime v 1905–1906 g.g.', *Krasnyi Arkhiv*, vol. 3, 1925, p. 5.
32 Kokovstov, *Out of My Past: Memoirs of Count Kokovtsov*, p. 462.
33 Ibid., pp. 459–60.
34 Ibid., p. 465.
35 Alexander Gerschenkron, *Europe in the Russian Mirror* (Cambridge: Cambridge University Press, 1970), p. 19.
36 James Mavor, *An Economic History of Russia* (London: Dent & Son, 1925), vol. 2, pp. 378–9.
37 Gerschenkron, *Europe in the Russian Mirror*, pp. 21–37.
38 B.A. McDaniel, 'Institutional Destruction of Entrepreneurship through Capitalist Transformation', *Journal of Economic Issues*, June 2003, p. 497.
39 PRO, FO 881/5674, p. 13.
40 V.P. Litvinov-Falinskii, *Fabrichnoe zakonodatel'stvo i fabrichnaya inspektsiya v Rossii* (St Petersburg: Suvorin, 1904), p. 29.
41 M.I. Tugan-Baranovsky, *The Russian Factory in the 19th Century* (Illinois: AEA, 1970), p. xi.
42 Ibid., pp. 9–11.
43 Ibid., pp. 364–79.
44 Ibid., p. 396.
45 M.I. Tugan-Baranovsky, *Osnovy politicheskoi ekonomii* (Moscow: Rosspen, 1998), p. 129.
46 Ibid., p. 130.
47 M.I. Tugan-Baranovsky, 'Sostoyanie nashei promyshlennosti za desyatiletie 1900–1909 gg. i vidy na budushchee', in *Periodicheskie promyshlennye krizisy* (Moscow: Rosspen, 1997), pp. 487–8.
48 Trakhtenberg confirmed Tugan's view that the first outbreak of the international monetary crisis occurred in mid-1899 in Russia, with the German stock exchange following suit in April 1900. See I.A. Trakhtenberg, *Denezhnye krizisy* (Moscow: AN SSSR, 1963), p. 438.
49 Tugan-Baranovsky, 'Sostoyanie nashei promyshlennosti za desyatiletie 1900–1909 gg. i vidy na budushchee', pp. 497–500. The 1905 revolution had prompted the formation of the Council of Congresses of Industry and Trade as a forum to represent business interests. See White, *The Russian Revolution, 1917–21*, pp. 37–8.
50 Olga Crisp, 'Banking in the industrialisation of Tsarist Russia', in *Studies in the Russian Economy Before 1914*, pp. 140–2.
51 Tugan-Baranovsky, 'Sostoyanie nashei promyshlennosti za desyatiletie 1900–1909 gg. i vidy na budushchee', pp. 507–12.
52 Gatrell, *The Tsarist Economy*, p. 228.

53 M.I. Tugan-Baranovsky, 'Narodnoe khozyaistvo', *Rech'* (St Petersburg, 1914), p. 342.
54 Ibid., p. 349.
55 Gatrell and Davies pointed out how Minister of Finance Kokovtsov's success in controlling state debt after 1908 likely assisted the access of private borrowers to the money market, much domestic savings going into commercial banks as a consequence. R.W. Davies (ed.), *From Tsarism to the New Economic Policy* (London: Macmillan, 1990), pp. 149–50.
56 Lyashchenko, *History of the National Economy of Russia to the 1917 Revolution*, pp. 655–71.
57 Alexander Gerschenkron, *Economic Backwardness in Historical Perspective* (Cambridge, MA: Harvard University Press, 1962), p. 22.
58 R.W. Davies, Mark Harrison and S.G. Wheatcroft, *The Economic Transformation of the Soviet Union, 1913–45* (Cambridge: Cambridge University Press, 1994), p. 3.
59 Tugan-Baranovsky, 'Narodnoe khozyaistvo', pp. 354–5.
60 Ibid., pp. 358–9.
61 Ibid., pp. 360–1.
62 Gerschenkron, *Europe in the Russian Mirror*, pp. 122–3.
63 Mavor, *An Economic History of Russia*, vol. 2, pp. 376–7.

## 3 Revolutionary economy

1 J.M. Keynes, *A Tract on Monetary Reform* (London: Macmillan, 1923), pp. 50–5.
2 James D. White, *The Russian Revolution, 1917–21* (London: Arnold, 1994), p. 50.
3 PRO, CAB/27/189/14, p. 2.
4 Ibid., p. 3
5 *Agrarnaya politika Sovetskoi vlasti, 1917–18* (Moscow: AN SSSR, 1954), pp. 56–7.
6 Rudolf Hilferding, *Finance Capital* (London: RKP, 1981), pp. 323–4.
7 Nikolai Bukharin, *Imperialism and World Economy* (London: Merlin, 1987), p. 69.
8 M.S. Atlas, *Natsionalizatsiya bankov v SSSR* (Moscow: GosFinIzdat, 1948), p. 92.
9 *Direktivy KPSS i sovetskogo pravitel'stva po khozyaistvennym voprosam*, vol. 1, p. 27.
10 Quoted in E.H. Carr, *The Bolshevik Revolution, 1917–23* (London: Macmillan, 1952), vol. 2, p. 9.
11 Atlas, *Natsionalizatsiya bankov v SSSR*, p. 89.
12 White, *The Russian Revolution, 1917–21*, pp. 185–7.
13 Atlas, *Natsionalizatsiya bankov v SSSR*, p. 92.
14 *Direktivy KPSS i sovetskogo pravitel'stva po khozyaistvennym voprosam*, vol. 1, p. 37.
15 White, *The Russian Revolution, 1917–21*, p. 222.
16 G.G. Shvittau, *Revolyutsiya i narodnoe khozyaistvo v Rossii* (Leipzig: Central, 1922), p. 81.
17 *Velikaya oktyabr'skaya sotsialisticheskaya revolyutsiya: entsiklopediya* (Moscow: SovEntsik, 1987), p. 330.
18 Silvana Malle, *The Economic Organisation of War Communism* (Cambridge: Cambridge University Press, 1985), p. 68.
19 *Agrarnaya politika Sovetskoi vlasti, 1917–18*, p. 152.

20 S.N. Prokopovich, *The Economic Condition of Soviet Russia* (London: King and Son, 1924), p. 39.
21 Shvittau, *Revolyutsiya i narodnoe khozyaistvo v Rossii*, p. 82.
22 Robert Lifman, *Formy predpriyatii kooperatsiya i sotsializatsiya* (Berlin: Obelisk, 1924) pp. 202–18.
23 B.M. Unterberger (ed.), *American Intervention in the Russian Civil War* (Lexington: Heath, 1969), p. 49.
24 Laszlo Szamuely, *First Models of the Socialist Economic Systems* (Budapest: Kiado, 1974), pp. 10–16.
25 White, *The Russian Revolution, 1917–21*, pp. 220–2.
26 Ian D. Thatcher, *Trotsky* (London: Routledge, 2003), pp. 105–7.
27 Anthony Heywood, *Modernising Lenin's Russia* (Cambridge: Cambridge University Press, 1999).
28 L.N. Yurovsky, 'Problems of a Moneyless Economy', in Alec Nove and I.D. Thatcher (eds), *Markets and Socialism* (Aldershot: Elgar, 1994), pp. 63–73.
29 P.A. Klein, 'Economics: Allocation or Evaluation?', in Warren J. Samuels (ed.), *The Economy as a System of Power* (New Jersey: Transaction, 1989).
30 N. Rubinshtein, *Sovetskaya Rossiya i kapitalisticheski gosudarstva v gody perekhoda ot voiny k miru* (Moscow: GosIzdat, 1948), p. 12.
31 PRO, T1/12602/24126/20, p. 1.

## 4 Bolshevik economy

1 R.W. Davies, *The Soviet Economy in Turmoil, 1929–30* (London: Macmillan, 1989), p. 43.
2 V.I. Lenin, 'The Tax in Kind', *Collected Works* (London: Lawrence & Wishart, 1965), vol. 32, pp. 334–5.
3 E.H. Carr, *The Bolshevik Revolution, 1917–23* (London: Macmillan, 1952), vol. 2, pp. 282–3.
4 *The Official Report of the British Trades Union Delegation to Russia in November and December 1924* (London: TUC, 1925), pp. 43–7.
5 Arup Banerji, *Merchants and Markets in Revolutionary Russia, 1917–30* (London: Macmillan, 1997).
6 S.A. Fal'kner, 'Proshloe i budushchee russkoi emissionnoi sistemy', *Sotsialisticheskoe khozyaistvo*, no. 2–3 (April–May) 1923, pp. 54–7.
7 Ibid., pp. 66–7.
8 See N.D. Kondratiev, 'Industriya i sel'skoe khozyaistvo i ikh vziamootnoshenni', *Trudy Zemplana* (Moscow, 1928), no. XIV.
9 A.V. Chayanov, 'On the Theory of Non-Capitalist Economic Systems', in *The Theory of Peasant Economy* (Homewood: Irwin, 1966), p. 23.
10 Alexander Chayanov, *The Theory of Peasant Cooperatives* (London: Tauris, 1991), pp. 20–2.
11 A. Bogdanov, *Essays in Tektology* (California: Intersystems, 1984), p. 3.
12 Ibid., p. 41.
13 N.I. Bukharin, 'New Course in Economic Policy', in *Selected Writings on the State and the Transition to Socialism* (New York: M.E. Sharpe, 1982), p. 126.
14 Ibid., p. 141.
15 Ibid., p. 113.
16 N.I. Bukharin, 'Concerning the New Economic Policy and Our Tasks', in *Selected Writings on the State and the Transition to Socialism*, p. 189.
17 N.I. Bukharin, 'The Road to Socialism and the Worker-Peasant Alliance', in *Selected Writings on the State and the Transition to Socialism*, p. 260.
18 Ibid., p. 261.

19 Ibid., p. 204.
20 E.A. Preobrazhensky, *The New Economics* (Oxford: Clarendon, 1965), p. 168.
21 Ibid., p. 171.
22 Ibid., p. 173.
23 L.N. Yurovskii, 'K probleme plana i ravnovesiya v sovetskoi khozyaistvennoi sistema', in *Finansovoe ozdorovlenie ekonomiki: opyt NEPa* (Moscow: Kaz'min 1990), p. 178.
24 Ibid., p. 179.
25 Ibid., p. 184–5.
26 Ibid., p. 188.
27 Ibid., pp. 201–2.
28 Ibid., pp. 206–8.
29 Ibid., p. 211–12.
30 Ibid., p. 214.
31 Ibid., p. 215.
32 Ibid., p. 221.
33 V.A. Bazarov, 'On the Methodology for Drafting Perspective Plans', in N. Spulber (ed.), *Foundations of Soviet Strategy for Economic Growth* (Indiana: Indiana University Press, 1964), p. 367.
34 Ibid., p. 371.
35 V.A. Bazarov, '"Krivie razvitiya" kapitalisticheskogo i sovetskogo khozyaistva', *Planovoe khozyaistvo*, no. 4, 1926, p. 107.
36 Ibid., pp. 110–14.
37 S.G. Strumilin, 'Sotsial'nie problemy pyatiletki', in *Izbrannie proizvdeniya* (Moscow: AN SSSR, 1963), vol. 2, p. 339.
38 Ibid., p. 340.

## 5  Stalinist economy

1 R.W. Davies, Mark Harrison and S.G. Wheatcroft (eds), *The Economic Transformation of the USSR, 1913–45* (Cambridge: Cambridge University Press, 1994), pp. 137–8.
2 M.I. Tugan-Baranovsky, *Sotsializm" kak" polozhitel'noe uchenie* (Petrograd: Koop, 1918), p. 101.
3 Ibid., pp. 104–5.
4 M.I. Tugan-Baranovsky, *K Luchshemy budushchemu* (Moscow: Rosspen, 1996), p. 352.
5 Silvana Malle, *The Economic Organisation of War Communism* (Cambridge: Cambridge University Press, 1985), pp. 304–5.
6 Thorstein Veblen, *The Engineers and the Price System* (New York: Viking, 1921), p. 139.
7 V.I. Lenin, *Collected Works* (London: L&W, 1965), vol. 32, p. 139.
8 E. Zaleski, *Planning for Economic Growth in the Soviet Union* (North Carolina: North Carolina Press, 1971), p. 38, Table 1.
9 Ibid., p. 143.
10 Naum Jasny, *Soviet Economists of the Twenties* (Cambridge: Cambridge University Press, 1972), p. 170.
11 *Ob edinom khozyaistvennom plane* (Moscow: Ekonomika, 1989), p. 23.
12 Ibid., p. 95.
13 E. Zaleski, *Stalinist Planning for Economic Growth* (North Carolina: North Carolina Press, 1980), p. 49.
14 As quoted in R.W. Davies, *The Soviet Economy in Turmoil, 1929–30* (London: Macmillan, 1989), p. 238.

15 Davies, *The Soviet Economy in Turmoil, 1929–30*, pp. 199–200.
16 *Direktivy KPSS i sovetskogo pravitel'stva po khozyaistvennym voprosam*, (Moscow: GosIzdat, 1957), vol. 2, pp. 336–7.
17 Ibid., p. 390.
18 PRO, FO 371/22293, pp. 63–7.
19 Davies, Harrison and Wheatcroft (eds), *The Economic Transformation of the USSR*, p. 292.
20 Holland Hunter and Janusz Szyrmer, *Faulty Foundations: Soviet Economic Policies, 1928–40* (Princeton: Princeton University Press, 1992), p. 245.
21 W.A. Lewis, *The Principles of Economic Planning* (London: Dobson, 1950), p. 110.
22 For example see Yu. Shirlin, 'Izuchenie potrebitel'skogo sprosa i predvaritel'nye zakazy', *Planovoe khozyaistvo*, no. 7, 1935, pp. 79–93.
23 Shirlin concluded that the study of consumer demand was a matter both for trading organisations themselves, and for government bodies such as Gosplan and NKVnuTorg. The structure and capacity of demand would be determined by the latter, the precise assortment of products by the former. See Shirlin, 'Izuchenie potrebitel'skogo sprosa . . .', p. 83. It is necessary to point out that the custom of Soviet planners genuinely seeking to fulfil the wants of consumers as measured in the way outlined by Shirlin was not standard practice in the USSR in the 1930s.
24 L.V. Kantorovich, *The Best Use of Economic Resources* (Oxford: Pergamon, 1965), pp. 2–3.
25 *Direktivy KPSS i sovetskogo pravitel'stva po khozyaistvennym voprosam*, vol. 2, p. 84.
26 Davies, Harrison and Wheatcroft (eds), *The Economic Transformation of the USSR*, pp. 120–3.
27 D.W. Treadgold, *Twentieth Century Russia* (Chicago: Rand, 1964), pp. 270–1.
28 R.W. Davies, *The Soviet Collective Farm* (London: Macmillan, 1980), p. 68.
29 Davies, *The Soviet Economy in Turmoil*, p. 261.
30 S.N. Prokopovich, *The Economic Condition of Soviet Russia* (London: King and Son, 1924), pp. 45–6.
31 Ibid., pp. 59–60.
32 John Dewey, *The Later Works, 1925–53* (Illinois: Carbondale, 1984), vol. 3, p. 221.
33 John Dewey, *The Later Works, 1925–53* (Illinois: Carbondale, 1984), vol. 5, p. 237.
34 A.A. Berle and G.C. Means, *The Modern Corporation and Private Property* (New York: Harcourt, 1968).
35 Ian D. Thatcher, *Trotsky* (London: Routledge, 2003), pp. 167–9.
36 J.M. Keynes, *Treatise on Money* (London: Macmillan, 1930), vol. 2, p. 386.
37 J.M. Keynes, *The General Theory of Employment, Interest and Money* (London: Macmillan, 1936), p. 378.
38 Keynes Papers, King's College, Cambridge, RV/1/38.
39 Keynes Papers, King's College, PS/5/109.
40 Keynes Papers, King's College, PS/5/112.
41 Gerschenkron, *Europe in the Russian Mirror*, p. 121.
42 PRO, FO 371/22293, p. 75.
43 Boris Brutzkus, *Economic Planning in Soviet Russia* (London: Routledge, 1935), p. 194 and pp. 231–4.

## 6 Conclusions for future economy

1 Wilhelm Reich, *The Mass Psychology of Fascism* (New York: Farrar, 1970), p. 221.
2 J.W. Hallcock, *Production Planning* (New York: Ronald Press, 1929), p. 3.
3 J.K. Galbraith, *The New Industrial State* (London: Hamilton, 1967), pp. 25–6.
4 F.A. Hayek, *Individualism and Economic Order* (London: RKP, 1976), pp. 78–9.
5 For example in Malcolm Bradbury's novel *The History Man*, the sociologist Howard Kirk employed socialist ideas for self-serving aims, the sexual conquest of students, seen by him as a 'perk of the job'. Readers might come to their own conclusions as to whether this is the behaviour of a genuine socialist.
6 Those libertarians who feel that all this sounds far to constricting should note that this conception would apply only to ground rules, not to specific actions. The 'grey areas' of social convention in which some types of people thrive sometimes only provides cover for cruel manipulation and exploitation.

# Bibliography

## Archive sources – English

Keynes Papers, King's College, Cambridge.
Public Records Office (PRO), Kew, London.

## Russian language sources – history

*Agrarnaya politika Sovetskoi vlasti, 1917–18* (Moscow: AN SSSR, 1954).

Atlas, M.S., *Natsionalizatsiya bankov v SSSR* (Moscow: GosFinIzdat, 1948).

*Direktivy KPSS i sovetskogo pravitel'stva po khozyaistvennym voprosam*, vol. 1 and vol. 2 (Moscow: GosIzdat, 1957).

Finn-Enotaevskii, A., *Kapitalizm v Rossii, 1890–1917* (Leningrad: NKFin, 1925).

'K peregovoram Kokovtsova o zaime v 1905–1906 g.g.', *Krasnyi Arkhiv*, vol. 3, 1925.

Lifman, Robert, *Formy predpriyatii kooperatsiya i sotsializatsiya* (Berlin: Obelisk, 1924).

Litvinov-Falinskii, V.P., *Fabrichnoe zakonodatel'stvo i fabrichnaya inspektsiya v Rossii* (St Petersburg: Suvorin, 1904).

*Ob edinom khozyaistvennom plane* (Moscow: Ekonomika, 1989).

'Otchet Kokovtsov komitetu finansov', *Krasnyi Arkhiv*, vol. 3, 1925.

Rubinshtein, N., *Sovetskaya Rossiya i kapitalisticheski gosudarstva v gody perekhoda ot voiny k miru* (Moscow: GosIzdat, 1948).

Shvittau, G.G., *Revolyutsiya i narodnoe khozyaistvo v Rossii* (Leipzig: Central, 1922).

Trakhtenberg, I.A., *Denezhnye krizisy* (Moscow: AN SSSR, 1963).

*Velikaya oktyabr'skaya sotsialisticheskaya revolyutsiya: entsiklopediya* (Moscow: SovEntsik, 1987).

## Russian language sources – economics

Bazarov, V.A., ' "Krivie razvitiya" kapitalisticheskogo i sovetskogo khozyaistva', *Planovoe khozyaistvo*, no. 4, 1926.

Chuprov, A.I., *Po povodu ukaza 9 Noyabrya 1906* (Moscow: Sabashnikov, 1908).

Fal'kner, S.A., 'Proshloe i budushchee russkoi emissionnoi sistemy', *Sotsialisticheskoe khozyaistvo*, no. 2–3 (April–May) 1923.

Kondratiev, N.D., *Mirovoe khozyaistvo i ego kon"yunktury vo vremya i posle voiny* (Vologda: GosIzdat, 1922).

Kondratiev, N.D., 'Industriya i sel'skoe khozyaistvo i ikh vziamootnoshenni', *Trudy Zemplana* (Moscow, 1928), no. XIV.

Migulin, P.P., *Nasha bankovaya politika* (Kharkov: Gagarin, 1904).

Ozerov, I.Kh., *Ekonomicheskaya Rossiya eya finansovaya politika na iskhod XIX i v nachal XX veka* (Moscow: Kushnerev, 1905).

Pervushin, S.A., *Khozyaistvennaya kon'yunktura* (Moscow: Ekonomicheskaya zhizn, 1925).

Shirlin, Yu., 'Izuchenie potrebitel'skogo sprosa i predvaritel'nye zakazy', *Planovoe khozyaistvo*, no. 7, 1935.

Strumilin, S.G., 'Sotsial'nie problemy pyatiletki', in *Izbrannie proizvdeniya* (Moscow: AN SSSR, 1963), vol. 2.

Tugan-Baranovsky, M.I., 'Narodnoe khozyaistvo', *Rech'* (St Petersburg, 1914).

Tugan-Baranovsky, M.I., *Sotsializm" kak" polozhitel'noe uchenie* (Petrograd: Koop, 1918).

Tugan-Baranovsky, M.I., *Kluchshemy budushchemu* (Moscow: Rosspen, 1996).

Tugan-Baranovsky, M.I., 'Sostoyanie nashei promyshlennosti za desyatiletie 1900–1909 gg. i vidy na budushchee', in *Periodicheskie promyshlennye krizisy* (Moscow: Nauka, 1997).

Tugan-Baranovsky, M.I., *Osnovy politicheskoi ekonomii* (Moscow: Rosspen, 1998).

Yurovskii, L.N., 'K probleme plana i ravnovesiya v sovetskoi khozyaistvennoi sistema', in *Finansovoe ozdorovlenie ekonomiki: opyt NEPa* (Moscow: Kaz'min, 1990).

## English language sources – Russian studies

Banerji, Arup, *Merchants and Markets in Revolutionary Russia, 1917–30* (London: Macmillan, 1997).

Bogdanov, A., *Essays in Tektology* (California: Intersystems, 1984).

Bukharin, N.I., 'New Course in Economic Policy', in *Selected Writings on the State and the Transition to Socialism* (New York: M.E. Sharpe, 1982).

Carr, E.H., *The Bolshevik Revolution, 1917–23* (London: Macmillan, 1952).

Carr, E.H., *What is History?* (Harmondsworth: Penguin, 1961).

Clark, Colin, *A Critique of Russian Statistics* (London: Macmillan, 1939).

Crisp, Olga, *Studies in the Russian Economy Before 1914* (London: Macmillan, 1976).

Davies, R.W., *The Soviet Collective Farm* (London: Macmillan, 1980).

Davies, R.W., *The Soviet Economy in Turmoil, 1929–30* (London: Macmillan, 1989).

Davies R.W., (ed.), *From Tsarism to the New Economic Policy* (London: Macmillan, 1990).

Davies, R.W., Mark Harrison and S.G. Wheatcroft (eds), *The Economic Transformation of the Soviet Union, 1913–45* (Cambridge: Cambridge University Press, 1994).

Davies, R.W., *Soviet Economic Development from Lenin to Khrushchev* (Cambridge: Cambridge University Press, 1998).

Emmons T., and W. Vucinich (eds), *The Zemstvo in Russia* (Cambridge: Cambridge University Press, 1982).

Engels, Frederick, 'Anti-During', in Alec Nove and I.D. Thatcher (eds) *Markets and Socialism* (Aldershot: Elgar, 1994).

Falkus, M.E., *The Industrialisation of Russia* (London: Macmillan, 1972).

Gatrell, Peter, *The Tsarist Economy, 1850–1917* (London: Batsford, 1986).

Gatrell, Peter, *Government, Industry and Rearmament in Russia* (Cambridge: Cambridge University Press, 1994).

Gerschenkron, Alexander, *Europe in the Russian Mirror* (Cambridge: Cambridge University Press, 1970).

Gerschenkron, Alexander, *Economic Backwardness in Historical Perspective* (Cambridge, MA: Harvard University Press, 1962).

Heywood, Anthony, *Modernising Lenin's Russia* (Cambridge: Cambridge University Press, 1999).

Hunter, Holland and Janusz Szyrmer, *Faulty Foundations: Soviet Economic Policies, 1928–40* (Princeton: Princeton University Press, 1992).

Jasny, Naum, *Soviet Economists of the Twenties* (Cambridge: Cambridge University Press, 1972).

Kahan, Arcadius, *The Plow, the Hammer and the Knout* (Chicago: Chicago University Press, 1985).

Kahan, Arcadius, *Russian Economic History* (Chicago: Chicago University Press, 1989).

Kayden E.M., and A.N. Antsiferov, *The Cooperative Movement in Russia During the War* (New Haven: Yale University Press, 1929).

Kokovtsov, V.N., *Out of My Past: Memoirs of Count Kokovtsov* (Stanford: Stanford University, 1935).

Kornai, Janos, *Vision and Reality, Market and State* (New York: Harvester, 1990).

Kotsonis, Yanni, *Making Peasants Backward* (London: Macmillan, 1999).

Lenin, V.I., *Collected Works* (London: Lawrence & Wishart, 1960), vol. 3.

Lenin, V.I., *Collected Works* (London: Lawrence & Wishart, 1965), vol. 32.

Lyashchenko, P.I., *History of the National Economy of Russia to the 1917 Revolution* (New York: Macmillan, 1949).

Malle, Silvana, *The Economic Organisation of War Communism* (Cambridge: Cambridge University Press, 1985).

Mavor, James, *An Economic History of Russia* (London: Dent & Son, 1925).

Mosse, W.E., *An Economic History of Russia* (London: Tauris, 1996).

*The Official Report of the British Trades Union Delegation to Russia in November and December 1924* (London: TUC, 1925).

Ol', P.V., *Foreign Capital in Russia* (New York: Garland, 1983).

Prokopovich, S.N., *The Economic Condition of Soviet Russia* (London: King and Son, 1924).

Smele, J.D., 'White Gold: The Imperial Russian Gold Reserve in the Anti-Bolshevik East', *Europe-Asia Studies*, vol. 46, no. 8.

Sokolnikov, Gregory, *Soviet Policy in Public Finance* (Stanford: Stanford University, 1931).

Szamuely, Laszlo, *First Models of the Socialist Economic Systems* (Budapest: Kiado, 1974).

Thatcher, Ian D., *Trotsky* (London: Routledge, 2003).

Treadgold, D.W., *Twentieth Century Russia* (Chicago: Rand, 1964).

Unterberger B.M., (ed.), *American Intervention in the Russian Civil War* (Lexington: Heath, 1969).

Waldron, Peter, *The End of Imperial Russia* (London: Macmillan, 1997).

White, James D., *The Russian Revolution, 1917–21* (London: Arnold, 1994).

White, James D., *Lenin* (London: Palgrave, 2001).

Zaleski, E., *Planning for Economic Growth in the Soviet Union* (North Carolina: North Carolina Press, 1971).

Zaleski, E., *Stalinist Planning for Economic Growth* (North Carolina: North Carolina Press, 1980).


## English language sources – economics

Bazarov, V.A., 'On the Methodology for Drafting Perspective Plans', in N. Spulber (ed.), *Foundations of Soviet Strategy for Economic Growth* (Indiana: Indiana University Press, 1964).

Berle A.A., and G.C. Means, *The Modern Corporation and Private Property* (New York: Harcourt, 1968).

Brutzkus, Boris, *Economic Planning in Soviet Russia* (London: Routledge, 1935).

Bukharin, Nikolai, *Imperialism and World Economy* (London: Merlin, 1987).

Chayanov, Alexander, 'On the Theory of Non-Capitalist Economic Systems', in *The Theory of Peasant Economy* (Homewood: Irwin, 1966).

Chayanov, Alexander, *The Theory of Peasant Cooperatives* (London: Tauris, 1991).

Dmitriev, V.K., *Economic Essays on Value, Competition and Utility* (Cambridge: Cambridge University Press, 1974).

Eltis, Walter, 'Harrod-Domar Growth', in *The New Palgrave Dictionary of Economics* (London: Macmillan, 1987), vol. 2.

Fusfeld, D.R., 'The Development of Economic Institutions', *Journal of Economic Issues*, December 1977.

Galbraith, J.K., *The New Industrial State* (London: Hamilton, 1967).

Hallcock, J.W., *Production Planning* (New York: Ronald Press, 1929).

Hayek, F.A., *Individualism and Economic Order* (London: RKP, 1976).

Rudolf Hilferding, *Finance Capital* (London: RKP, 1981).

Howard M.C., and J.E. King, *A History of Marxian Economics* (Princeton: Princeton University Press, 1989).

Kantorovich, L.V., *The Best Use of Economic Resources* (Oxford: Pergamon, 1965).

Katzenellenbaum, Z.S., *Russian Currency and Banking* (London: King and Son, 1925).

Keynes, J.M., *Treatise on Probability* (London: Macmillan, 1921).

Keynes, J.M., *A Tract on Monetary Reform* (London: Macmillan, 1923).

Keynes, J.M., *Treatise on Money* (London: Macmillan, 1930).

Keynes, J.M., *The General Theory of Employment, Interest and Money* (London: Macmillan, 1936).

Klein, P.A., 'Economics: Allocation or Evaluation?', in Warren J. Samuels (ed.), *The Economy as a System of Power* (New Jersey: Transaction, 1989).

Kornai, Janos, *Anti-Equilibrium* (Amsterdam: North-Holland, 1971).

Lewis, W.A., *The Principles of Economic Planning* (London: Dobson, 1950).

McDaniel, B.A., 'Institutional Destruction of Entrepreneurship through Capitalist Transformation', *Journal of Economic Issues*, June 2003.

North, D.C., *Structure and Change in Economic History* (New York: Norton, 1981).

Preobrazhensky, E.A., *The New Economics* (Oxford: Clarendon, 1965).

Rostow, W.W., *The Stages of Economic Growth* (Cambridge: Cambridge University Press, 1971).

Rostow, W.W., *Theorists of Economic Growth from David Hume to the Present* (Oxford: Oxford University Press, 1990).

Schumpeter, Joseph, *Business Cycles* (New York: McGraw-Hill, 1939).

Schumpeter, Joseph, *Imperialism and Social Classes* (Oxford: Blackwell, 1951).

Screpanti, Ernesto and Stefano Zamagni, *An Outline of the History of Economic Thought* (Oxford: Clarendon, 1993).

Solo, R.A., *Economic Organizations and Social Systems* (Ann Arbor: University of Michigan Press, 2000).

Sundrum, R.M., *Economic Growth in Theory and Practice* (London: Macmillan, 1990).

Tugan-Baranovsky, M.I., *The Russian Factory in the 19th Century* (Illinois: AEA, 1970).

Veblen, Thorstein, *The Engineers and the Price System* (New York: Viking, 1921).

Yurovsky, L.N., 'Problems of a Moneyless Economy', in Alec Nove and I.D. Thatcher (eds), *Markets and Socialism* (Aldershot: Elgar, 1994).

Wiles, P.J.D., *Communist International Economics* (Oxford: Blackwell, 1968).

## English language sources – philosophy

Dewey, John, *The Later Works, 1925–53* (Carbondale: Illinois, 1984), vol. 3.

Dewey, John, *The Later Works, 1925–53* (Carbondale: Illinois, 1984), vol. 5.

Lenin, V.I., *Materialism and Empirio-Criticism* (Moscow: Progress, 1947).

Lewis, David, *On the Plurality of Worlds* (Oxford: Blackwell, 1986).

Reich, Wilhelm, *The Mass Psychology of Fascism* (New York: Farrar, 1970).

Wittgenstein, Ludwig, *Tractatus Logico-Philosophicus* (London: RKP, 1981).

# Name index

# Subject index